THE
ELEVEN-PLUS
BOOK

Martin Stephen is former High Master of St Paul's School, London, and prior to that was High Master of The Manchester Grammar School, only the second man in history to hold both posts. He is the author of numerous academic books on English literature and history, and of the four novels in the acclaimed Henry Gresham series of historical crime thrillers. His latest book is *The Diary of a Stroke*. He is married to Jenny, former headmistress of South Hampstead High School, and has three adult sons.

THE ELEVEN-PLUS BOOK

GENUINE EXAM QUESTIONS
FROM YESTERYEAR

FOREWORD BY
DR MARTIN STEPHEN
FORMER HIGH MASTER, ST PAUL'S SCHOOL

Michael O'Mara Books Limited

This paperback edition first published in 2016

First published in Great Britain in 2008 by
Michael O'Mara Books Limited
9 Lion Yard
Tremadoc Road
London SW4 7NQ

Copyright © Michael O'Mara Books Limited 2008, 2013, 2016

A CIP catalogue record for this book is available from the British Library.

Papers used by Michael O'Mara Books Limited are natural, recyclable
products made from wood grown in sustainable forests. The
manufacturing processes conform to the environmental regulations of
the country of origin.

ISBN: 978-1-78243-507-5 in paperback print format
ISBN: 978-1-84317-737-1 in Epub format
ISBN: 978-1-84317-738-8 in Mobipocket format

1 2 3 4 5 6 7 8 9 10

Designed and typeset by Martin Bristow

Printed and bound by CPI Group (UK) Ltd, Croydon, CR0 4YY

www.mombooks.com

CONTENTS

FOREWORD

The Eleven-Plus was born out of the 1944 Butler Education Act, which used the test to decide if a child would go to the academically selective grammar schools, or in the case of failure, to a technical or a secondary modern school. My mother inherited a large stone house in Sheffield, surrounded by one of that city's bigger council housing estates. Fear of the Eleven-Plus should have stalked the streets of that estate: the ruthless examination that quietly culled the bright working-class children. But the young people I knew had an almost subliminal expectation that their role in life was to go to the secondary modern school (which has since been replaced by the comprehensive school). Was it therefore an exam for the middle class? Well, my highly middle-class brother failed it, and I knew plenty of other middle-class children who didn't make the grade. So was the Eleven-Plus an exam that failed both the working and the middle classes? It is certainly the most maligned exam in the history of UK education. The mere mention of it is sufficient to provoke violence among left wing and liberal opinion, and it has become the symbol of the longest and most bitter educational war ever fought in this country, namely the war over selection.

It is a war where both sides have a point. Feminists missed a trick when they failed to adopt the Eleven-Plus as one of their symbols of male dominance. Marks had to be fiddled in order to give more grammar school places to boys; the girls did too well at the Eleven-Plus, both for the number of places available and for the attitude of the times to women. Furthermore, the whole structure whereby the Eleven-Plus was marked was based on the supposition that academic ability was in turn based on a 'normal curve of distribution', i.e. a few people at the top and a few at the bottom, with most spread on a spectrum of ability in the middle – a bell-shaped curve, in effect. The problem was that no one had ever proved that academic ability was distributed this way.

A further problem was the relatively primitive nature of some of the tests used in the Eleven-Plus. I well remember being ranked as educationally sub-normal (something many people might agree with) on one of these tests. It showed five shapes, and asked which one was the odd one out. The answer was the one that was not based on a triangle. My answer was based on the fact that four of the shapes resembled medieval axe-heads, and one did not. I was rather miffed at being told I was stupid when I thought (and still think) my answer was better than the examiner's.

Yet one thing shines clear down the ages about the Eleven-Plus for me. When I went up to university in Leeds in 1967, it was full of working-class and maintained-school pupils who had got there through the Eleven-Plus. Whatever evils it may have contained, the Eleven-Plus was the agency whereby huge sectors of English society had the chance of a good university degree opened up to them. It may have caused a lot of casualties, but the Eleven-Plus won a battle in the war of access that our generation appears to be losing.

Dr Martin Stephen
Former High Master, St Paul's, 2008

EDITOR'S NOTE

The Eleven-Plus has waned severely in popularity since its inception in the 1940s, and today is used in only a handful of boroughs and counties in England, though more widely in Northern Ireland.

The examination was set by Local Education Authorities in the United Kingdom, and as a result differed in format from region to region. The exam questions we have compiled in this book come from various LEAs, and include entrance exam questions from the 1940s and 1950s. Most Eleven-Plus papers had at least three set constituents – Arithmetic, General Intelligence (sometimes called General Problem Solving or, more commonly now, General Knowledge), and some form of English paper. We have therefore included sections on Arithmetic, General English, Comprehension, General Intelligence, and finally a section on Essays and Compositions. We included this last section so you can see the sort of questions that were asked, and, if you're feeling creative, you can have a go; but obviously we could not supply set answers for these, so why not mark each other? Don't be too harsh, though: it's just for fun!

For the Comprehension and Essay and Compositions questions you would have been given a list of questions from which you would answer two or three in the time allocated. So instead of grouping these in examination papers, we've just listed various questions for you to choose from. Similarly, the General Intelligence section is one group of questions rather than a number of papers, simply because of the large number of questions you were expected to answer – to include a few examination papers would have trebled the length of the book!

Because the Eleven-Plus differed in structure in each area of the United Kingdom, the time allocated for exam papers and the marking systems were not consistent across the country. Consequently we have not stipulated a set time in which to answer the questions, though as a guide the Arithmetic and General English papers would normally take 1 to 1½ hours each; and instead of using a marking system we have simply provided the answers so you can compare with your friends and family as to who managed to answer most correctly. There were in fact no grades awarded for the Eleven-Plus: it was simply a case of pass or fail, and of course depended on how many places were actually available in the local grammar, secondary modern and technical schools.

We hope you enjoy getting competitive with your friends and family members as you tackle *The Eleven-Plus Book*, and discover whether you can meet the standards of the eleven-year-olds of yesteryear!

ARITHMETIC

EXAMINATION 1

1. Simplify:

   (a) 15×20

   (b) $\frac{1}{2} + \frac{1}{3}$

   (c) 0.75×3

2. Write in figures the sum of ninety-five and four hundred and eleven.

3. A train leaves London at 11.30 a.m. and arrives at Bristol at 1.30 p.m., after stopping from 12.10 p.m. to 12.20 p.m. at Reading, which is 36 miles from London. It travelled both parts of the journey at the same rate. Find the distance from London to Bristol.

4. Out of a £6,000 donation, £1,000 was given as prizes to a local school, and half the remainder was given to charity. The rest was divided amongst 4 children. How much did each get?

5. Mary is 12 years old and her father is 42. Answer these questions:

   (a) How old was Mary's father when he was 4 times as old as Mary?

   (b) In how many years' time will her father be 3 times as old as Mary?

   (c) How old will Mary be when her father is 10 times as old as Mary was 6 years ago?

6. A machine makes tin boxes at the rate of 78 in 5 minutes. How long will it take to make 3,900 of them? (Answer in hours and minutes.)

7. If 1st December falls on a Friday, on what day will Christmas Day fall that year?

8. A library has 2,672 'A' books and 5,172 'B' books. During the year in 'A' section 514 new books are bought, 398 are moved to 'B' section, and 23 are lost. In 'B' section, 297 are sent to salvage or lost. How many are there in each section at the end of the year?

9. There were 9,975 spectators at a football match. This is 5 per cent more than were present at the preceding match. How many attended the previous match?

10. How many seconds are there between 11.53 a.m. and 12.18 p.m. the same day?

EXAMINATION 2

1. Write in figures:

   Seven hundred and three thousand three hundred and seventy.

2. (a) What number must be added to the sum of 14 and 15 to make 40?

   (b) Find the sum of all the odd numbers between 10 and 20.

3. A rice pudding was placed in the oven at a quarter to eleven and taken out at half-past twelve. For how many minutes was it in the oven?

4. A man bought 500 lettuce plants and after planting 12 rows with the same number in each, he had 32 left over. How many were in each row?

5. A church bell rings once every 6 seconds and the bell of a nearby church rings once every 8 seconds. If they start ringing together, after how many seconds do they next ring together?

6. Four boys, each having the same number of marbles, started playing games. At the end of all the games, Albert had 22 marbles, Bob had 33, Charles had 20 and Dan had 41. How many marbles had each won or lost?

7. (a) Multiply 6,195 by 780

   (b) Divide 15,867 by 369

8. Seven piles of bricks are placed side by side so that their tops form steps 1 brick high. If the lowest pile contains 9 bricks, how many bricks are being used altogether?

9. A contractor agrees to complete a house in 250 days, and to do this he engages 60 men. After 200 days no work is done for 10 days. How many extra men must he engage to finish the house in time?

10. A man looks at his watch as he starts from home for his office, and the time is 7 minutes past 8. He walks 6 minutes to a bus stop, and waits 3 minutes for the bus. The journey takes 11 minutes, and when he gets off the bus he could walk to his office in 2 minutes; but he stops to talk to a friend for 4 minutes. When he gets to the office, the office clock says 20 minutes to 9. Is the clock slow or fast by his watch, and by how much?

EXAMINATION 4

1. Multiply 2,098 by 79, and without further working write the answer of 1,049 × 79.

2. (a) Multiply the sum of 4.5 and 7.58 by their difference.

   (b) Divide the sum of 2³⁄₁₀ and 4¼ by their difference.

3. Three times a certain number is 107 more than 343. What is that number?

4. A page of a book has 35 lines of print on it. Each complete line has an average of 11 words in it, but 4 of the lines have only 6 words in them and 1 line has only 3 words. How many words are there on the page?

5. A football match begins at 2.10 p.m. The teams play for 40 minutes, have a rest of 5 minutes at half time, and play again for another 40 minutes. At what time will the match finish?

6. An aeroplane took off at 5.20 p.m. and reached its destination 300 miles away at 6.50 p.m. What was its speed in miles per hour?

7. From Monday to Friday a man works from 7.45 a.m. to 12.15 p.m., and from 1.15 p.m. to 5.45 p.m. On Saturday he works in the morning only from 7.45 a.m. to 1 p.m., and on Sundays he does not work at all. There is 20 minutes' rest every morning and a quarter of an hour in the afternoon. How many hours does the man work in a week?

8. An aeroplane flying in a straight line at 300 miles per hour passes over 'A', and 12 minutes later passes over 'B'. What is the distance between 'A' and 'B'?

9. I have two watches. One gains 3 minutes every 6 hours whilst the other loses 2 minutes every 4 hours. If I set both watches right at 7.30 a.m. on Monday, how many minutes' difference will they show at 7.30 p.m. (correct time) on Tuesday?

10. There are 35 pupils in a class; 0.6 of them are girls. How many are boys?

EXAMINATION 5

1. ⅗ + ⅔ hours. Give the answer in minutes.

2. If 17 × 13 is 221, what is 1.7 × 0.13?

3. A ship has enough food to last a crew of 45 men for 32 days. How long would the food last if the crew consisted of only 40 men?

4. A factory employs 1,044 people: ¼ of them cycle to work, ½ of them travel by bus. Of the remainder, ⅓ come by the train and the others walk. How many walk to work?

5. The sun sets at 4.53 p.m. on a certain day and rises at 7.36 a.m. the next morning.

   (a) The street lamps were lit half an hour after sunset. What time were they lit?

   (b) The street lamps were put out half an hour before sunrise. What time were they put out?

   (c) How long were the lamps alight during the night?

6. My watch gains 30 seconds every hour. If I set it at the correct time at 9 a.m. on Monday, what time will it be on my watch when the correct time is 9 a.m. on Thursday?

7. A gardener started to plant 10 rows of cabbage plants at 10.15 a.m. He planted the first 6 rows at the rate of 5 rows in 25 minutes, and the last 4 rows at the rate of 3 rows in 33 minutes. At what time did he finish the 10 rows?

8. If 1st January is on a Saturday, on what day of the week is 31st January?

9. After spending 0.35 of my money, what decimal fraction have I left?

10. In the number 953, how much greater is the 9 than the 5?

EXAMINATION 6

1. 3,755 is multiplied by 25 and the result is divided by 125. Write down the answer.

2. 565 is the correct answer when 3 numbers are added up: one of them is 89, another is 286. So what is the third?

3. (a) How many seconds are there between 11.47 a.m. and 1.07 p.m.?

   (b) A bus starts on a journey at 10.25 a.m. If the journey takes 100 minutes, when will it arrive?

4. An orchard contained 87 trees in 8 lines with the same number of trees in each line except the last, which was short. How many trees were there in the last line?

5. A motorist leaves home at 10.15 a.m. and drives at 32 miles per hour. He stops for lunch from 12 noon to 1.45 p.m. and then continues his journey at 30 miles per hour. How many miles has he travelled by 5 p.m.?

6. A second-hand car was sold for £273. This was 6/7 of its cost when new. What was paid for it when new?

7. A father leaves £3,200 to be shared among 6 sons and 4 daughters. Each son is to receive twice as much as a daughter. What will each son receive?

8. How many minutes does a car travelling at 45 miles per hour take for 24 miles?

9. A man covers 5/8 of a journey by train and 1/6 by boat. His train journey is 44 miles longer than that by boat. What is the length of the whole journey?

10. Fred had a bag of counters; ⅓ were red and the rest were white. Harry had as many counters as Fred, but ⅓ of his was white and the rest were red. They mixed the counters and took ½ of them. After this, Harry had 7 red counters for every 5 white counters. What fraction of Fred's counters was red?

EXAMINATION 7

1. Divide 460,731 by 59.

2. Express as a decimal the difference between ⅘ and 0.75.

3. An aeroplane uses 100 gallons of petrol for a flight of 150 miles. How far could it fly using 40 gallons?

4. A cyclist sets out at 8.30 a.m. and rides at 12 miles per hour. He stops from 12 noon until 1 p.m. for lunch, and from 4 p.m. until 4.30 p.m. for tea. He reaches the end of his journey at 6.30 p.m. How many miles has he travelled?

5. £125 a second was raised during the Savings Campaign. How much was raised in 3 minutes?

6. A boy going to school walks for 32 minutes at the rate of 2½ miles an hour. Then fearing to be late he runs the rest of the way in 3 minutes at 6 miles an hour. How far has he to travel to school?

7. I have 40 marbles. I lose 0.2 of them and give away 0.5 of the remainder. How many marbles have I left?

8. An aeroplane travelling at 300 miles per hour passes over Edinburgh and flies straight to Glasgow, which it reaches 8 minutes later. What is the distance between the two cities?

9. (a) Multiply 687 by 208.   (b) Divide 28,782 by 39.

10. A newsreel cinema opened at 2 p.m. From 2 p.m. to 3 p.m., 410 people entered and 86 people left. From 3 p.m. to 4 p.m., 257 people entered and 207 left. From 4 p.m. to 5 p.m., 156 entered and 396 left. How many people were inside at 5 p.m.?

EXAMINATION 8

1. Write out the following in figures and add them up:

   Two hundred and four thousand and nine; seventy thousand, nine hundred and eight; four hundred and fifty thousand and seventy; one hundred and seven thousand, three hundred and ninety-five.

2. (a) Divide seventeen thousand, eight hundred and fifteen by thirty-five.

   (b) $13.7 - 6.79 + 0.3 - 1.22$

3. Mary's height is 4 ft 10 in. Ethel is 4 inches taller than Mary. How tall is Ethel?

4. On opening a box containing 6 dozen eggs, it was found that 23 were broken. How many whole eggs remained?

5. A clock, which loses ½ a minute every hour, is put right at 9 a.m. on Monday. What time will it show at 9 a.m. on Wednesday?

6. In a school there are twice as many girls as there are boys. 50% of the boys and 25% of the girls are under 11 years of age. If there are 486 children in the school how many of them are *not* under the age of 11 years?

7. The result in an election was as follows:

Brown	7,361
Jones	5,972
Smith	2,667

   (a) How many people voted?

   (b) If there were 18,000 people who could have voted, what proportion did vote?

(c) If Smith had not put up for election, and all his votes had gone to Jones, who would have won the election, and by how many votes?

8. I have 80 marbles. I lose 0.3 of them and give away 0.25 of the remainder. How many have I left?

9. Share 100 sweets between 2 children, giving one 30 more than the other.

10. A meeting started at 10.50 a.m. and lasted 2¾ hours. At what time did it finish?

EXAMINATION 9

1. Write in figures: twelve thousand and twelve.

2. (a) (6¾ of 4⅔) – (10⅚ ÷ 11⁄12)   (b) 1.06 × 2.04 ÷ 0.12

3. A race started at 23 minutes past 3 and finished at 23 minutes to 4. How long did it take?

4. A boy did 20 mental sums in 25 minutes. If he continued at the same rate, how many did he do in 1 hour?

5. The road from a town 'A' to another town 'B' is uphill for the first 2 miles, level for the next 3 miles, and downhill for the last 2 miles. If I can walk at the rate of 4 miles an hour on the level, 5 miles an hour downhill and 3 miles an hour uphill, how long shall I take to go from 'A' to 'B'?

6. A train due to arrive at 9.50 a.m. was 45 minutes late. At what time did it arrive?

7. There are 98 boys and 102 girls in a school. There is 1 teacher for every 40 children. How many teachers are there?

8. Three cases contain 789 tins of sardines. In one there are 267 tins and in another 63 more than in the first. How many tins does the third case contain?

9. Find the sum of all the numbers between 1 and 13 that are divisible exactly by 3.

10. A clock is 12 minutes slow, but is gaining 5 seconds per hour. A watch is 20 minutes fast, but is losing 7½ seconds per hour. How many minutes fast will the watch be when the clock shows the right time?

EXAMINATION 10

1. Simplify:

   (a) 1,000 – 10

   (b) 25 × 12

   (c) 615 ÷ 3

   (d) 0.5 + 0.75

   (e) ⅘ – ⁷⁄₁₀

2. What is the smallest number greater than 500 that is divisible by 11?

3. A car travels at 48 miles an hour. How far does it go in 40 minutes?

4. John's age is 12 years and 9 months. William is 18 months older than John. What is William's age?

5. Two trains connect with each other every day at a junction. Train 'A' leaves a town 176 miles away at 9 a.m. and averages 48 miles per hour. Train 'B' leaves a town 98 miles away at 10 a.m. and averages 30 miles per hour.

   (a) Which is the first train to reach the junction and at what time does it arrive?

   (b) How long would a passenger on it have to wait for the other train to arrive?

6. A cyclist leaves place 'A' at 1 p.m. to cycle to place 'B' 42 miles away. He arrives there at 4.30 p.m. At what time must a motor-cyclist, travelling 3 times as fast as the cyclist, leave 'A' to arrive at 'B' at the same time?

7. In an election, 3 candidates, Brown, Green and White, receive a total of 36,820 votes. Green has 580 more than White. Brown has twice as many as Green. How many has Brown?

8. If 24th November is a Saturday, what day is 10th December?

9. A train runs from London to Glasgow in 11 hours at the rate of 35 miles an hour. How long would it take if the speed were to be increased by 5 miles an hour?

10. How does a timetable show this time: thirteen minutes to ten in the evening?

EXAMINATION 11

1. Simplify:

   (a) 4.7×100 (b) $4.7 \div 100$ (c) 6×0.7 (d) $2.4 \div 6$

2. (a) 'A' owns 0.18 of a business; 'B' owns 0.125 of it; 'C' 0.375; and 'D' the rest. Find 'D''s share.

   (b) If the whole business is worth £10,000, find the value of 'D''s share.

3. Divide 0.18 by 0.3

4. A train travels at 44 miles an hour. How far will it go in 45 minutes?

5. The average of 4 men's ages is 30 years, while the average age of 3 of them is 33 years. What is the age of the fourth man?

6. A train due at 5.43 a.m. arrived at 6.27 a.m. How many minutes was it late?

7. (a) What time is it 87 minutes after 10.42 a.m.?

   (b) Change 8,640 minutes to days

8. An aeroplane flies from Glasgow to London in 1 hour 51 minutes at 220 miles per hour. Find the distance in miles.

9. Which is the largest of these fractions: $\frac{7}{12}$, $\frac{3}{4}$, $\frac{2}{3}$?

10. How much less than 12 is the number that is 3 more than 4?

EXAMINATION 12

1. Simplify:

  (a) $1\frac{1}{2} + 1\frac{1}{3} + 1\frac{1}{6}$ (b) $10 - 3\frac{9}{10}$ (c) $8 \times \frac{1}{8}$

  (d) $20 \div 2\frac{1}{2}$ (e) $4.8 \div 0.1$

2. Add all the odd numbers between 12 and 20.

3. Multiply the sum of 10.3 and 0.98 by their difference.

4. A game begins at 2.35 p.m. Halfway through there is a 10-minute rest. If the playing time is 80 minutes, at what time did the game end?

5. Add: 4,568
           1,796
             957
           2,745

6. A train leaves London at 10.35 a.m. and arrives at Birmingham at 1.50 p.m. How many minutes does the journey take?

7. A holiday resort has continuous sunshine from 9.42 a.m. to 5.13 p.m. on a certain day. How many minutes was that?

8. A cyclist rode 8 miles in 32 minutes. How many miles an hour was this?

9. A man was born in 1891 and died in 1927. How old was he when he died?

10. In a game James scored 4 points for every 3 points Mary scored. The total was 140 points. How many of these did Mary score?

EXAMINATION 13

1. Simplify:

    (a) 13 + 27 + 36   (b) 83 – 37   (c) 28,133 ÷ 7

    (d) 7,236 × 5,287   (e) ½ + ¼ + ⅞

2. How long would it take to go 100 miles at 15 miles an hour?

3. Simplify:

    (a) 29 + 16 – 8   (b) ⅝ – ¼   (c) 3.4 + 1.6

4. A man is packing eggs in boxes, each of which holds 56. When he has packed all the eggs, he finds he needs 2 more to fill 32 boxes. How many eggs does he have?

5. Mr Rose walked ½ mile on Monday, twice as far on Tuesday as on Monday, twice as far on Wednesday as on Tuesday, and so on all the week. How far did he manage to walk on Saturday?

6. How long would it take to go 57 miles at 12 miles an hour?

7. In a bag of beads ¼ of them are red, ½ of them are white and 42 are blue. How many beads does the bag contain?

8. Which of these numbers is divisible by 4 without any remainder: 214, 230, 226, 224, 218?

9. One day ⅖ of the boys from a school were at home ill. If 84 were in school, how many stayed at home?

10. If a motorcar covers a distance of 42 miles in 1½ hours, how long at the same rate should it take to complete a journey of 147 miles?

EXAMINATION 14

1. Multiply 7,296 by 479.

2. There are 120 children in a school. If the number of girls is 8 more than the number of boys, how many boys are there?

3. (a) $7.42 - 0.156 + 8.007$ (b) $258.4 - 29.62$

4. Find the number of days from 23rd November 1950 to 7th January 1951, including both these dates.

5. I want to visit my friend who lives on a farm 4½ miles off. If I wish to arrive at a quarter to one, in time for dinner, what time must I leave home if I walk at the rate of 3 miles an hour?

6. A man starts on a journey of 6 miles at 11.50 a.m. After walking the first mile in 13 minutes he covers the rest of the journey in a car that is travelling at 30 miles an hour. When does he arrive?

7. Of 800 people living in a village, half are men and half women. A quarter of the men leave the village to join the army. How many more women than men now remain?

8. Work out:

   (a) Divide ½ by 5 (b) $0.0048 \div 0.8$ (c) $5\frac{1}{7} \times 10\frac{1}{2} \div 3\frac{3}{8}$

9. A clock gains ½ a second every hour. It is correct at noon on Monday. On what day will it be exactly 1 minute fast?

10. A colony contains 30,000 people, made up of English, Dutch and natives, in equal numbers. Each year the English lose $\frac{1}{10}$ of their numbers and the natives add $\frac{1}{10}$ to their numbers. The Dutch remain unchanged. What will be the population of the colony at the end of 2 years?

EXAMINATION 15

1. (*a*) Write in figures: ten thousand seven hundred and five

   (*b*) Add 9,378 to 5,063

   (*c*) From 4,580 take 2,667

   (*d*) Divide 5,427 by 9

2. Divide 2,262 by 78.

3. How many times does the minute hand of a clock travel round the clock face in a week?

4. Twice one hundred and sixty-eight added to four times another number gives a total of four hundred and eighty. What is the other number?

5. Write down all the simple factors (prime factors) of 165.

6. (*a*) Write down the lowest common multiple of 6, 9 and 12.

   (*b*) Write down the prime (simple) factors of 210.

   (*c*) What are the next three numbers to follow: 25, 19, 14, 10 . . . ?

7. The distance from 'X' to 'Y' is 28 miles. At 8 a.m., 'A' sets out from 'Y' to walk to 'X' at the speed of 4 miles an hour. At 10 a.m., 'B' sets out from 'X' to bicycle to 'Y' at 10 miles an hour. How far from 'Y' will 'A' and 'B' meet?

8. (*a*) 23.6 + 0.94 + 2.78

   (*b*) 28 – 9.63

   (*c*) 81,027 ÷ 9

9. A train leaving 'A' at 8.38 a.m. is timed to reach 'B' at 3.22 p.m. Ten minutes after the arrival of this train another one leaves 'B' for 'A'. These two trains do the journeys in the same time; so at what time is the train from 'B' expected to be in 'A'?

10. One motor-car, travelling at 30 miles an hour, leaves London at the same time as another car travelling at 25 miles an hour leaves a certain town. When the two cars meet, one has travelled 20 miles more than the other. What is the distance from this town to London?

GENERAL ENGLISH

EXAMINATION 1

1. Replace the word underlined by one with the opposite meaning:

    (a) The defeat of the French

    (b) The soldier's bravery

    (c) The exports of Canada

    (d) The day of his birth

    (e) A glorious sunset

    (f) My greatest friend

    (g) The experiment was a failure

    (h) The descent of the mountain

2. Put the following sentences into the plural, changing all necessary words:

    (a) My cat caught a mouse.

    (b) Her grocer has no butter.

    (c) This knife is very blunt.

    (d) A woman who lives in a shoe is sure to have trouble with her child.

3. Punctuate the following and insert capitals where necessary:

    towards october the bear came back my friends down there wish me to present their compliments he said and he picked some curious things out of his shaggy coat here you shall see what I have for you what is it asked the oak this is a beech nut answered the bear

4. Fill in the blanks in the following sentences with suitable words. There is no need to write the sentences out. Simply put the number of the sentence and after it write the word which you think is correct.

   (a) As *finger* is to *hand* so is .... to *foot*.

   (b) As *den* is to *fox* so is .... to *bees*.

   (c) As *Spain* is to .... so is *France* to *Frenchmen*.

   (d) As *ounce* is to *weight* so is *inch* to ....

   (e) As *umpire* is to *tennis* so is .... to *football*.

   (f) *Construction* is exactly opposite in meaning to de ....

   (g) *Dw* .... is exactly opposite in meaning to *giant*.

   (h) *Beauty* is exactly opposite in meaning to *ug* ....

   (i) *So* .... is exactly opposite in meaning to *joy*.

   (j) *Height* is exactly opposite in meaning to *de* ....

5. Make each of these groups of sentences into one sentence without changing the meaning. Do not use the words 'and' or 'but'. The first one is done for you as an example.

   Example: The book was on the table. My mother told me to give it to her.

   Answer: My mother told me to give her the book that was on the table

   (a) My father bought me a bicycle. Its colour was green.

   (b) I saw a flower in your garden. It was red. It had a lovely scent.

   (c) We were not able to play football today. It was raining.

   (d) I could not walk along the lane. It was narrow. The snow had drifted into it.

EXAMINATION 2

1. Rewrite the following sentences, using only the correct word from each bracket:

   (a) (*Whose, Who's*) afraid of the big bad wolf?

   (b) (*Those, Them*) books are the ones I want to read.

   (c) I took a parcel to (*there, their*) house.

   (d) The dog can see (*its, it's*) master when (*its, it's*) standing by the gate.

   (e) She (*has, as*) forgotten (*where, were*) she put her knitting.

2. An ignorant man with bad handwriting took a page to a printer who did not know his job. This is what was produced:

   > 'in the eveaning I allways goes for a wak. Some time i see nothing interested but some time i do see something wurth describing. One neight ass I looked over the sea, I notised a strange lite and their was a bought full of german sellers; comin ashore. They was all very quite but I herd clerly the plash of their ors.'

   Write out the passage correctly.

3. Here are incorrect versions of common sayings; write each out correctly and say what you think the correct version means:

   (a) People who live in glass houses should not tell lies.

   (b) Rolling stones break no bones.

   (c) P.S. means: please excuse scribble.

   (d) A bird in the hand makes a mess.

4. Write out the following passage again, including only the *one correct* word from each bracket:

    The boy (who, whom, what) we met at the baths and (who, whom, what) spoke to (you, I, me) and (you, I, me) is Harry Baines; he (use, used) to live near me and he often (come, came, went) to my house to play with me. He had a good stamp collection; the total number of his stamps (are, was, were) more than three thousand. (He, Him, Me) and (I, him, me) (was, am, were) great friends.

5. Rewrite each sentence, putting *one* word only for each group of words underlined:

    (a) I was in no doubt that the door was locked.

    (b) I shall finish reading this book in a short time.

    (c) She made up her mind to go shopping.

    (d) He drove his car to the place where they sell petrol and oil.

    (e) He ran at a great pace to the station.

EXAMINATION 3

1. Rewrite the following paragraph, putting in all capital letters and punctuation marks that are needed:

   i saw mrs jones in the town this morning i said as i walked into the kitchen did you dear said mother and what did she say we didnt speak i replied she was busy shopping and i was in a hurry to get home.

2. Some words are missing from the following story. Write down the word that should be written in the place of each letter:

   Cinderella was a poor little girl who (a) with her two (b) step-sisters. They were very (c) to her and treated her (d) a servant. They made her look after (e) hand and (f), and she was (g) all the dirty work in the (h).

   One evening, a (i) ball was held in the palace of the (j) young prince. (k) the sisters were (l). (m) they put on their beautiful dresses, they made fun (n) Cinderella, who had no fine (o) and had not (p) invited to the ball.

   (q) Cinderella! After the sisters had (r), she sat (s) by the fire, crying (t) she was so unhappy.

3. Write one word which could replace the words under-lined in each of the following sentences:

   Example: The <u>covering on top of the pie</u> was broken. (Crust.)

   (*a*) He tripped his sister <u>although he did not mean to do it</u>.

   (*b*) <u>Afraid of nothing</u>, he went alone into the haunted room.

   (*c*) The mother <u>made</u> the frock <u>as good as new again</u>.

   (*d*) The doctor saved the life of the <u>person whom he attended</u>.

(e) The captain <u>made up his mind</u> to sail at dawn.

4. There is something wrong with each of the sentences given below. Write them as you think they should be written:

   (a) The chair was by the window on which he stood.

   (b) I'd rather an apple than a pear.

   (c) The strongest of the twins was the shortest.

   (d) It is difficult to divide one small apple between six people.

   (e) I asked him whether his name was William.

5. Give *one word* for each of the following phrases:

   (a) A place where aeroplanes land and take off.

   (b) A ship that travels under water.

   (c) An instrument that measures cold and heat.

   (d) A place where wild animals are kept for exhibition.

   (e) A piece of land where cultivated fruit trees are grown.

   (f) A man who draws and paints.

   (g) A large party of singers.

   (h) A stream that flows into a river.

   (i) A man who repairs frozen water pipes.

   (j) The twelve persons who decide whether the prisoner is guilty or not.

EXAMINATION 4

1. Copy this letter, setting it down in its proper form, and putting in any punctuation that is needed:

   62 Green Lane Aytown 2 January 1955 Dear Rose Thank you very much for your Christmas card and good wishes for the New Year I hope you had a very jolly time and that 1955 will be a very happy year for you I am looking forward to seeing you in the summer Your loving friend Beryl.

2. Write down a word opposite in meaning to each of the following:

   (*a*) clean

   (*b*) advance

   (*c*) useful

   (*d*) moisture

   (*e*) possible

   (*f*) weakness

   (*g*) shapeless

   (*h*) allow

   (*i*) absence

   (*j*) foolishness

3. Pick out the <u>verbs</u> from the following sentences and write them out in the <u>past tense</u>:

   (*a*) She teaches us to sing.

   (*b*) I see the mountain.

   (*c*) My friend brings his books home.

   (*d*) He holds the cards in his hand.

   (*e*) He cuts the cloth neatly.

4. Rewrite these sentences, putting *one* word only for each group of words underlined:

   (*a*) I live <u>within a stone's throw of</u> the school.

   (*b*) Mr Smith is <u>advanced in years</u>.

   (*c*) He seized the knife <u>before you could say Jack Robinson</u>.

   (*d*) He <u>could not remember</u> my address.

   (*e*) She did her sums <u>without any difficulty</u>.

5. Rewrite the following paragraph, putting in the necessary capitals and punctuation:

   sam weller took his hat and hastened to meet his father who on seeing his son approach said well im glad to see you sammy and how are you this morning

EXAMINATION 5

1. *Black* is the opposite of *white*; *long* is the opposite of *short*.
   Now write down the opposites of these words:

   (a) wide

   (b) bright

   (c) unkind

   (d) eatable

   (e) visible

   (f) evil

   (g) quickly

   (h) smooth

   (i) cheap

   (j) sour

2. Write these words in the correct order to make sentences:

   (a) had waited the until door I closed he

   (b) many with helped I his him homework have times

   (c) first year of always exciting I the the is day think

   (d) listened on programme the switched to wireless he and the

   (e) to asked a letter me she write

3. Give the feminine of each of the following:

   (a) brother

   (b) nephew

   (c) monk

(d) wizard

(e) gander

(f) merman

(g) waiter

(h) hero

(i) fox

(j) cousin

4. Rewrite the following sentences, using the plurals of the underlined words:

(a) The angry <u>goose</u> snapped at my bare <u>foot</u>.

(b) <u>This</u> young deer lived in yonder <u>valley</u>.

(c) The <u>police-constable</u> chased the <u>thief</u> across the <u>roof</u>.

(d) He will come for <u>you</u> but not for <u>me</u>.

5. Write down one word in place of each phrase underlined:

(a) The boy <u>made up his mind</u> to sell his bicycle.

(b) The girl tried <u>again and again</u> until she succeeded.

(c) The vehicle was <u>standing still</u>.

(d) The soldier was forced to <u>give himself up to the enemy</u>.

(e) My brother always comes to school <u>at the right time</u>.

(f) The soil is <u>not yielding any produce</u>.

(g) The firm's books were examined <u>every year</u>.

(h) Some animals are <u>not able to be seen</u> at night.

EXAMINATION 6

1. Give sentences of your own to express the meaning of *five* of the following:

   (*a*) John had jumped out of the frying pan into the fire.

   (*b*) He was caught red-handed.

   (*c*) It is best to make hay while the sun shines.

   (*d*) His bark is worse than his bite.

   (*e*) The boy is never stumped for an answer.

   (*f*) His excuse would not hold water.

2. Write these lines of poetry in the usual way, putting in capital letters and the correct punctuation:

   the evening is coming the sun sinks to rest the rooks are all flying straight home to the nest caw says the rook, as he flies overhead it's time little people were going to bed

3. Make adjectives from these nouns:

   beauty, slope, glass, friend, doubt, expense, delight, sleep, danger, sport.

4. Correct the following sentences:

   (*a*) A crate of apples have been hid by the thieves

   (*b*) Each of the men wears numbers on their shirts.

   (*c*) I will be drowned and no one shall save me.

   (*d*) The biggest of the two tigers sprung out of the cage.

   (*e*) That is the boy who I have spoke to you about.

5. Rewrite the following passage, substituting a more suitable word for 'nice' each time it occurs and using a different word in each case:

It was such a *nice* day that Jane and Peter decided to go for a *nice* walk. They had a *nice* breakfast, and their mother gave each of them a *nice* apple and a *nice* piece of cake. Off they went up the hill to the woods, passing several *nice* houses on the way. From the top of the hill they had a *nice* view of the countryside. Jane picked some *nice* flowers, while Peter looked for birds' nests.

EXAMINATION 7

1. Write short, clear sentences to illustrate the following points:

   (a) The word *long* used as an adjective.

   (b) *Long* used as a verb.

   (c) *Want* used as a verb.

   (d) *Want* used as a noun

   (e) *Up* used as an adverb.

   (f) *Night* used as an adjective.

   (g) *Haul* as a noun.

   (h) *Heat* as a verb.

2. Add a prefix to each of the following to make its meaning the opposite of what it is now:

   regular, capable, sense, legal, concerned.

3. Rewrite the following sentences, putting in all the punctuation marks and capitals required:

   (a) hurry shouted john the train is in. we have another minute his friend replied

   (b) is the honey good asked mr lion it is delicious replied the jackal

4. Write this sentence with each word on a separate line, and put opposite each one what part of speech (verb, adjective, etc.) it is:

   But the Giant immediately put them into his gloomy dungeon.

5. In each of the following sentences there are words that are not necessary to the sense. Write the sentences out, *leaving the unnecessary words out*:

(a) The Chairman stood up on his feet and made a long and lengthy speech.

(b) The old man had reached the advanced age of ninety-five.

(c) The early morning sun shone straight into his bedroom, which looked towards the east.

(d) The young girl had grown to her full height and would never be any taller.

(e) They saw the birds again in the evening towards the close of day.

EXAMINATION 8

1. Write this story as if the third boy were telling a friend what had occurred.

   Two boys found a nut. Both claimed it, one because he saw it first, the other because he picked it up. They asked a third boy who was passing by to decide whose it was. He cracked the nut and gave half the shell to each boy, saying that he would take the kernel himself as his fee for acting as a judge.

2. Write a suitable answer to each of these questions. Do not answer with just one or two words, but make up a good sentence.

   (a) How is your mother today?

   (b) Have you hidden the scissors?

   (c) When would you like to come and have tea with me?

   (d) Why is George sitting on the floor?

   (e) Who is the lady in the fur coat?

3. What is the plural of these nouns?

   (a) boy

   (b) egg

   (c) bench

   (d) ox

   (e) box

   (f) enemy

   (g) hare

   (h) hair

   (i) fish

   (j) sheep

4. Arrange the following sentences to form a complete paragraph:

These are made by stretching seal-skins over a light wooden frame.

On the Arctic coasts of North America live the Eskimos.

Their hunting is done by means of boats called kayaks.

Because of their light weight, the boats are easily carried across the ice.

They exist mainly on seals and fish, which they catch in summer.

5. Underline the one word among the four on the right, which best describes what has been written on the left. Here is an example:

The King's coronation

event; happening; sight; <u>ceremony</u>

(a) A bad railway crash

mistake; accident; fault; event

(b) A place where travellers can eat and sleep

house; restaurant; hotel; mansion

(c) Uncertain news passed on from one person to another

rumour; information; chatter; talk

(d) Someone you know just well enough to speak to when you meet him

acquaintance; friend; companion; stranger

EXAMINATION 9

1. Rewrite the following, putting in all the paragraphs, capital letters, necessary stops, inverted commas, and other punctuation marks:

> son son said his mother waving her tail now attend to me and remember what i say a hedgehog curls himself up into a ball and his prickles stick out every way at once by this you may know the hedgehog i dont like this old lady a bit said Stickly Prickly i wonder what else she knows a tortoise cant curl himself up mother jaguar went on by this you may know the tortoise

2. We talk of a football *pitch*. What special names are connected with these games and pastimes?

> a golf ....   a skating ....   a race ....
> a tennis ....   a bowling ....

3. (*a*) These words express movement:

> *galloped, trudged, crawled, raced, trotted*

Arrange them according to speed, beginning with the slowest.

(*b*) These words express sound:

> *rumbled, whispered, boomed, murmured, thundered*

Arrange them in order beginning with the weakest sound.

4. Rewrite the following sentences, using only the correct word from each bracket:

(*a*) Several people (swam, swum) the Channel this year.

(*b*) My brother and (I, me) went to the football match.

(*c*) I (seen, saw) her with my own eyes.

(*d*) The policeman knew (whom, who) had broken the window

(*e*) None of the girls (was, were) there in time.

5. (*a*) Choose the best adjective from list A to go with each noun in list B.

(*b*) Then write five sentences, each containing one of the pairs you have made.

A	B
muddy	mistake
exciting	walk
careless	boots
bitter	adventure
brisk	wind

EXAMINATION 10

1. Write down the names by which we call the following:

   (*a*) A soldier who is placed on guard.

   (*b*) A book containing a record of happenings day by day.

   (*c*) A period of a hundred years.

   (*d*) The followers of Mussolini.

   (*e*) The place where sick or injured people are taken.

   (*f*) A vehicle to carry sick or injured people.

   (*g*) A man whose wife is dead.

   (*h*) A fertile spot in a desert.

   (*i*) A practice trial of a play before actual performance.

   (*j*) Birds which fly away in autumn.

2. Draw a line under each verb and two lines under each adverb:

   I thoroughly enjoyed our school concert this year. First the choir sang many songs beautifully and later the orchestra played well. I thought Susan Jenkins danced very gracefully and John Robins recited two exciting poems excellently. The top class acted a play superbly and the programme ended with us all singing heartily.

3. Rewrite the following sentences in the plural form throughout:

   (*a*) The boy is flying his kite in the field.

   (*b*) The pony was in the same meadow as the ox.

   (*c*) The girl's scarf was found in the box.

    (*d*) The trout lies motionless whilst its enemy watches it with great patience.

4. Describe in *one* sentence for each, the work done by:

    (*a*) a doctor

    (*b*) a cobbler

    (*c*) an architect

5. Rewrite the following, putting a better word for *nice* each time it occurs. Use a different word each time.

    Tom and Susan are two very *nice* children and their uncle, who is a *nice* man, thought it would be *nice* to invite them to his farm. They spent a very *nice* fortnight with him, and they would like a *nice* holiday like this every year.

EXAMINATION 11

1. Put each line of words in the best order to make a good sentence. Write out the sentences correctly:

   (*a*) school was morning he this for late.

   (*b*) the the at to crossroads she right turned.

   (*c*) care your to take book blot not.

   (*d*) me help way please my find to.

   (*e*) will the people coming many concert to be.

2. Explain in your own words the meanings of the phrases printed in *italics*:

   (*a*) There is *no love lost* between Frank and Joe.

   (*b*) David is always *getting into hot water*.

   (*c*) Her singing *sets my teeth on edge*.

   (*d*) His name is *on the tip of my tongue*.

   (*e*) Harry looks as though he is *on his last legs*.

3. There are errors in these sentences. You are asked to rewrite them correctly:

   (*a*) Him and his sister went to the pictures.

   (*b*) The girl said she done it herself.

   (*c*) One of the thieves were caught.

   (*d*) Give me them oranges.

   (*e*) The man learnt to swim.

   (*f*) The lady sings quite nice.

   (*g*) He did not except the handsome present.

   (*h*) Neither one or the other is correct.

(*i*) I was that breathless I could hardly speak.

(*j*) A more kinder man never lived.

4. 'Blue' and 'blew' have the same sound, but are different in meaning. For each word below write another which has the same sound:

(*a*) reads

(*b*) might

(*c*) fourth

(*d*) serf

(*e*) mail

(*f*) wears

(*g*) mussel

(*h*) waist

5. Rewrite the following sentences, putting a suitable word in each blank space:

(*a*) He was very interested .... my story.

(*b*) His cap is a different colour .... mine.

(*c*) She walked gaily .... the road.

(*d*) Teacher was very pleased .... my work.

(*e*) I seized him .... the throat.

EXAMINATION 12

1. Rewrite this passage in the present tense – that is, as if it were happening now. When you have finished, make sure that it reads sensibly.

    I thought it was time for Bill to go home and told him so. Bill put on his hat and coat, opened the door and ran down the path. When he came to the gate, he stopped for a moment and turned. Then he threw the ball back to me.

    'Here,' he said, 'you can keep this.'

2. Read the following sentences and decide which is the correct word in each bracket. Write down the word:

    (a) He (past, passed) the house on (is, his) way to the station.

    (b) I shall ask teacher if I (may, can) leave early.

    (c) (Those, Them) are the people (who's, whose) car was stolen.

    (d) (His, Is) friends (were, wear) always saying he was (to, too) fat.

    (e) The (to, two) girls walked (passed, past) me with (there, their) heads in the air.

3. Complete each of the following sentences with an interesting phrase.

    Example: Wander to those mountains that sparkle like strange, sad jewels.

    (a) The bodies of the soldiers lay like ....

    (b) The sky is as clear as ....

    (c) The day dawned like ....

    (d) There was a silence like ....

    (e) They were sleeping as if ....

4. Here is a short composition. The first sentence is in its proper place, but the other sentences are mixed up. Write out the composition correctly:

Mr and Mrs Smith have three children.
The other two are Peter and Doris.
She likes it very much and works hard.
The eldest is Susan, who is twelve.
They are twins and are nine years old.
Now, she has just started at a new school.
Last year, she passed her examination.

5. The phrases on the right are similar in meaning to the words on the left. Write in a column the letters (a) to (h), which are given with the words. Opposite each letter, put the number of the phrase that is similar in meaning.

Example: (a) 5

(a) faithful	1. all of a flutter
(b) dislike	2. like a bear with a sore head
(c) while	3. with one's nose in the air
(d) irritable	4. for ever and a day
(e) haughty	5. as good as one's word
(f) always	6. afraid of one's shadow
(g) timid	7. in the course of
(h) excited	8. take exception to

EXAMINATION 13

1. Rewrite the following as eight lines of poetry. Put in all the capital letters and punctuation marks that are required:

   the swallow oft beneath my thatch shall twitter from her clay-built nest oft shall the pilgrim lift the latch and share my meal a welcome guest around my ivied porch shall spring each fragrant flower that drinks the dew and lucy at her wheel shall sing in russet gown and apron blue.

2. Below are five pairs of sentences. Join each pair into one sentence, using one of these words each time:

   who   whom   whose   which

   (a) The shells are pretty. I found them on the shore.

   (b) The policeman spoke to the man. The man was standing by the lamp-post.

   (c) Mr and Mrs Johnson are very pleasant people. Their son is my best friend.

   (d) I could not find the boy. I was looking for him.

   (e) Mrs White has gone abroad. I have known her for many years.

3. Write the correct form of the word in brackets in the following sentences (write the word only, not the full sentence):

   (a) She has (teach) for years.

   (b) Where has he (go)?

   (c) Many birds have (fly) over this field.

   (d) Have you (sew) the buttons?

   (e) Three rabbits were (shoot) last night.

(f) The bell has (ring).

(g) He did not know the man (who) I saw.

(h) Here is the boy (who) book I borrowed.

(i) Yesterday I (can) not see him, but I (find) him this morning.

4. The following are answers to questions. Make up a good question for each answer and write it down:

(a) It is hanging up in the cupboard.

(b) Because I was tired of waiting.

(c) That is the new teacher.

(d) As soon as I have eaten my dinner.

(e) About ten or twelve inches.

5. Choose the correct word from those in brackets:

(a) She gave the (fare, fair) to the conductor.

(b) I am (confidant, confident) of success.

(c) Why does she (die, dye) her hair?

(d) His sister has (wrote, written) him a letter.

(e) The screw fell off because it was (lose, loose).

EXAMINATION 14

1. Rewrite the following using *one* word instead of each group of words underlined:

   <u>Boys and girls</u> who go to the <u>building where books are kept</u> must be <u>on their best behaviour</u>. If they are not the <u>man who is in charge of the books</u> will send them out <u>at once</u>. All the <u>people who borrow books</u> must <u>bring back</u> the books within fourteen days or else they are <u>asked to pay a fine of</u> one penny. Books must be kept <u>free from dirt</u> when they are being read. Books can be borrowed only <u>if you agree to</u> these conditions.

2. In each bracket in the following sentences is an incorrect form of the verb. Write out the sentences correctly.

   Example: The ship (*sink*) after striking the rocks.
   Sentence: The ship *sank* after striking the rocks.

   (*a*) I asked if he had (*do*) his homework.

   (*b*) I have (*tear*) my coat on a nail.

   (*c*) He has (*fall*) off the ladder and hurt himself.

   (*d*) We (*go*) to the door but found she had (*go*).

   (*e*) They (*run*) away when I shouted to them.

3. Rewrite the following passage, putting in the necessary punctuation marks and capital letters:

   how will you know your uncles house mary asked me as far as i remember i replied its a white green tiled house i believe a house called the willows is next door

4. Rewrite the following sentences, using only the correct word from each bracket:

   (a) There (is, his) a cat on the lawn and I think (it's, its) ours.

   (b) She (lay, laid) on the bed for a rest.

   (c) There (were, where) no other people in the field (were, where) we had our picnic.

   (d) Tom and Jim both write well, but Tom is the (more, most) careful of the (too, two) boys.

   (e) She had to (practice, practise) on the piano every day.

5. Rewrite the following sentences, using only the correct word from each bracket:

   (a) Each of you (shouts, shout) loudly but neither of you (speak, speaks) clearly.

   (b) (Does, Do) Tom and his brother know that Mary and her mother (were, was) kept waiting?

   (c) Either the cat or the dog (is, are) sleeping, for neither the mouse nor the rat (run, runs) away.

   (d) We do not care to (who, whom) you give the presents so long as you do not give them to Bob and (she, her).

   (e) Tell (me, I) the answer and I shall tell (she, her).

   (f) After the mill-worker had (wove, woven) the cloth, she found it had (shrunk, shrank).

EXAMINATION 15

1. From what nouns (naming words) are these verbs formed:

   (a) fly

   (b) sing

   (c) give

   (d) think

   (e) bear

2. Write out the following sentences, filling the blank spaces with the most suitable word from those in brackets:

   (a) My name is different .... yours (than, as, from, to).

   (b) The poor woman had a .... shawl over her head (woollen, wooden, iron, feather).

   (c) .... do you consider the best scholar in our school? (who, whom, what, whose).

   (d) The .... boy was very kind to his parents (clever, stupid, tall, affectionate).

   (e) The king with his generals .... at the ceremony yesterday (is, are, was, were).

   (f) The plant that comes up out of the ground every year without replanting is a .... (annual, perennial, everlasting, evergreen).

   (g) The master of a merchant ship is known as a .... (colonel, grocer, captain, salesman).

   (h) The crew of the aeroplane fortunately escaped without .... (reward, punishment, opposition, injury).

(i) The poor fellow was .... and quite unable to move (ungrateful, generous, paralysed, feverish).

(j) A great mass of snow tumbling down a hillside is a .... (landslide, earthquake, avalanche, tornado).

3. All the following sentences have mistakes in them. Rewrite the sentences correctly:

   (a) Jim and me seen him do it.

   (b) None of my books are very exciting.

   (c) He has dropped the plate and broke it.

   (d) Me and Mary done our homework together.

   (e) Where are them people going?

4. Two of the following six sentences could be the second sentence of a composition, which starts with the sentence underlined. Write out the two sentences:

   Aunt Ethel is very fond of pets.
   She went to the shop to buy dog biscuits.
   Her house is always full of cats.
   She does not like dogs or cats.
   She put a saucer of milk under the table.
   She has two cats, a dog and a parrot.
   She will not let them come into the house.

5. Write out the following, putting in necessary capital letters and punctuation:

   At four o'clock Margaret and john turned the corner They gazed with wonder. what had they seen In front of their fathers house stood a brand new car. What a beautiful car exclaimed John who was jumping with joy.

EXAMINATION 16

1. Fill in the relative pronoun in the following sentences:

    (a) That is the coat .... my brother took away.

    (b) The man to .... I spoke was very disagreeable.

    (c) The boy .... ball I kicked was offended.

    (d) The man .... does his duty is always brave.

    (e) He asked me .... I intended to do.

2. (a) Form nouns from the following verbs:
    sell, buy, consume, imagine.

    (b) Form verbs from the following nouns:
    proof, refusal, variety, provision.

    (c) Form adjectives from the following nouns:
    rag, dream, perplexity, waste.

    (d) Write the plural form of these words:
    mummy, man-of-war, curio, crockery.

3. Rewrite these sentences, using the exact words of the speakers. Remember to put in all punctuation marks and capital letters needed.

    Example: I said that I was tired.
    Answer: 'I am tired,' I said.

    (a) Sally said that she was going to the pictures.

    (b) Tommy complained that his tooth was aching.

    (c) Mother told me to run for the doctor.

    (d) Mr Roberts remarked that I should have to wait for ten minutes.

    (e) Anne asked if she might borrow my pencil.

4. Choose the correct word from those in brackets and write it down. The first is done for you.

   Example: The gardener cut a (bow, bough) off the tree.

   Answer: bough

   (a) I hope you will be lucky (too, two).

   (b) He slid down the (shoot, chute) into the water.

   (c) He wore a (flour, flower) in his buttonhole.

   (d) A new (pane, pain) is needed in this broken window.

   (e) I arranged to (meet, meat) Tom in the park.

5. Complete the following sentences by putting in the right word – *one* word only:

   (a) They will arrive much .... early.

   (b) What time will be convenient .... you?

   (c) Great anxiety was felt .... his illness.

   (d) I live far .... my work.

   (e) Every detail is examined .... care.

   (f) This is the very person of .... we were speaking.

   (g) The roof is lower .... the steeple.

   (h) The embroidery was done .... hand.

   (i) She was .... reliable that everyone trusted her.

   (j) The Mistress was pleased .... the maid.

   (k) My idea of pleasure is different .... yours.

   (l) There is little difference .... your writing and mine.

   (m) The man .... car was damaged had disobeyed the traffic signals.

   (n) Neither of those pictures .... shown at the Plaza last week.

   (o) The lecturer was indignant .... the insults he received.

EXAMINATION 17

1. Select *one* adjective from the list to complete each sentence:

   polite, sarcastic, ravenous, modest, ungrateful.

   (*a*) A successful person who does not boast is
   ....

   (*b*) Someone who makes unkind and cutting remarks is ....

   (*c*) Someone who does not bother to thank you for helping him is ....

   (*d*) A boy who raises his hat to ladies is ....

   (*e*) Someone who is very hungry indeed is ....

2. Rewrite the following sentences in their correct form:

   (*a*) On the table was two long pipes.

   (*b*) I was tired, so I laid down.

   (*c*) He is as good as her.

   (*d*) The river don't run uphill.

   (*e*) Neither Holland nor France are rich in minerals.

   (*f*) The cat as well as the dog are white.

   (*g*) The good temper of the children charm me.

   (*h*) I suffer more from the quarrel than him.

   (*i*) Within the cell stands two cloaked figures.

   (*j*) He has just wrote to his father.

3. What is the special name given to the *money*:

   (*a*) your mother or father gives you each week to spend on yourself;

    (*b*) the shopkeeper returns to you if you pay him too much;

    (*c*) you pay to ride on a bus or train;

    (*d*) you collect in a box or bank to use later;

    (*e*) you earn for doing a job?

4. Write the following in your own words:

> . . . when I hear the squirrel
> Chitter-chattering to the sky,
> Then I know that Maytime
> And the warm days are nigh.

5. (*a*) Rewrite the following, using more interesting words for those underlined:

'It was a <u>nice</u> evening so I <u>got on</u> my bicycle and rode off into the country. When I <u>got to</u> the nearest village I <u>went to</u> my aunt who gave me a piece of <u>nice</u> cake and a glass of <u>nice</u> milk. Later, when I <u>got back</u> home, I felt very tired, so after a <u>nice</u> supper I went to bed and soon fell into a <u>nice</u> sleep.'

  (*b*) Write down a suitable word for each of the blank spaces in the following sentences. (Do not write the whole sentence.)

    (i) The river varied in breadth .... 50 to 100 feet.

    (ii) Presently the .... of water fell gently upon my ear.

    (iii) The fog was so thick that a powerful light was not .... at twenty yards.

    (iv) William drew my .... to the beautiful sunset.

    (v) He had never been in such a difficult .... before.

EXAMINATION 18

1. Rewrite these sentences so that you give the actual words used by the speakers.

   Example: I said that I was tired.
   Answer: 'I am tired,' I said.

   (a) He asked me where I was going.

   (b) I replied that I was going to the station.

   (c) She told her mother that she had lost her money.

   (d) He complained that the tea was cold.

2. Each of the following sentences contains one error. Rewrite the sentences correctly:

   (a) This is not an Infant's School.

   (b) I am told that Tom Jones's brother have won a Scholarship.

   (c) The bishop and another fellow then entered the hall.

   (d) When the dog recognised me it wagged it's tail.

   (e) That matter does not concern you or I.

   (f) Talking to my friend, the bus passed me.

3. Change all the words in the following sentences that are in the singular into the plural.

   Example: He put on his tie
   Answer: They put on their ties.

   (a) The monkey plays on the branch of the tree.

   (b) The lady has sliced the loaf and is peeling a potato.

   (c) He has put his scarf on.

(d) The old man sits on a bench in the shade.

(e) She has taken the goose to the pond.

4. Choose the correct word from those in brackets and write it down. The first is done for you.

Example: The procession was a fine (sight, site) to watch.

Answer: sight

(a) The roses in our garden have a lovely (scent, sent).

(b) A fire was burning in the (great, grate).

(c) The farmer has a fine (heard, herd) of cattle.

(d) She bought a new coat at the (sail, sale).

(e) The cold wind stung his (bare, bear) legs.

5. Write these lines in your own words:

Up and down the mower goes
All the long field over,
Cutting down the long green grass,
And the purple clover.

COMPREHENSION

EXAMINATION 1

1. Read the passage carefully and answer the questions below in your own words:

> Edward was forty-nine. He was a small, thin, stunted man, with a look of narrow cunning, of petty shrewdness. He had been clerk to Lawyer Ford for thirty-five years and had also furtively practised for himself. At the age of fourteen he sat in a grimy room with an old man on one side of him, a copying-press on the other, and a law-stationer's almanac in front, and he earned half a crown a week. At the age of forty-nine he still sat in the same grimy room and he earned thirty shillings a week. But now he, Edward, was the old man, and the indispensable lad of fourteen, who had once been himself, was another lad, perhaps thirtieth of the dynasty of office boys. Throughout this interminable period he had written the same letters, kept the same accounts, lied the same lies, and thought the same thoughts. In the eyes of the townspeople he was a decent fellow, a confirmed bachelor, an excellent clerk and a thrifty individual.

(a) How old was Edward when he started work with Lawyer Ford, and how long had he been at the job?

(b) 'Interminable' means 'endless'. What do you think made this period seem endless to Edward?

(c) How do you know that Edward lived before the present-day?

(d) What did people think of Edward?

(e) Was Edward married? How do you know?

(f) Explain in your own words the meaning of:

   (i) stunted

   (ii) furtively

   (iii) the indispensable lad

   (iv) a thrifty individual

2. Read the following passage carefully and then answer the questions in complete sentences:

Robin Hood spent his boyhood days on the edge of Sherwood Forest in the county of Nottingham. He grew up to be a strong and handsome youth, a skilful archer, quite happy and contented with his life near the greenwood and the company of his friends, chief of whom was his cousin Will.

But one sad day this peaceful life was disturbed, when Robin's home was suddenly attacked by enemies of his father. Robin and his friends defended the home with great bravery, but all in vain. The house was burnt to the ground, his father and several men were killed, and Robin himself barely escaped with his life. You can well understand how sad and bitter would be his thoughts as he fled from the ashes of his old home to the depth of Sherwood Forest.

Robin vowed to revenge himself on those who had robbed him of his father, his home, and his friends. He would live in the forest the life of an outlaw, he would rob the rich and give to the poor, he would gather round him bold and daring men like himself, he would feed on the King's deer, and merry should be his life in the forest glades.

(a) Where was Robin Hood brought up as a boy?

(b) What happened to change Robin's life?

(c) What is meant by he 'barely escaped with his life'?

   (d) Where did he go after his home had been burnt?

   (e) What is meant by 'he would feed on the King's deer'?

   (f) What kind of a man was Robin Hood?

3. Read the following story:

A Crow, having taken a bit of cheese out of a cottage window, flew into a high tree to eat it. A Fox, observing this, came and sat underneath, and began to praise the Crow's beauty.

'I have never observed it before,' he said, 'but your feathers are of a more delicate white than any I have seen in my life. And what a fine shape your body is! I am sure, too, that you have a beautiful voice. If it is as fine as your complexion, I do not know a bird that can compete with you.'

The bird wriggled with pleasure, but being a little uneasy about what the Fox said of her voice, thought she would show him how beautiful it really was. She began to sing and instantly the cheese dropped out of her beak. The Fox picked it up and trotted away, laughing to himself at the easy credulity of the Crow.

Now answer these questions in sentences:

   (a) Mention two untruths the Fox told.

   (b) How did the Fox get the cheese?

   (c) Where did the cheese, which the Crow had, come from?

   (d) The Fox laughed at the credulity of the Crow. What does this mean?

   (e) What lesson are we expected to learn from this story?

4. Read the following:

> 'You are old, Father William,' the young man said,
> 'And your hair has become very white;
> And yet you incessantly stand on your head –
> Do you think, at your age, it is right?'
> 'In my youth,' Father William replied to his son,
> 'I feared it might injure the brain;
> But, now that I'm perfectly sure I have none,
> Why, I do it again and again.'
> 'You are old,' said the youth, 'as I mentioned before,
> And have grown most uncommonly fat;
> Yet you turned a back-somersault in at the door –
> Pray, what is the reason of that?'
> 'In my youth,' said the sage, as he shook his grey locks,
> 'I kept all of my limbs very supple
> By the use of this ointment – one shilling the box –
> Allow me to send you a couple?'

Now answer these questions:

(a) Father William was certainly a queer man. Mention two queer things that he did.

(b) When he was young, Father William thought that one of his pranks might do him harm. When he was old, he changed his mind. Why?

(c) What does 'incessantly' mean? What is a back-somersault?

(d) What does the word 'supple' mean? How did Father William keep supple? Do you keep supple in the same way?

(e) What signs of old age did Father William show?

5. Read the following story from Aesop's Fables:

Belling the Cat

A large family of merry mice lived happily together in the cellar of a lofty house. Their only enemy was a fierce, black cat, who kept the mice in constant fear of a sudden and cruel death. Even in the dead of night it was not safe for them to stir far from their holes in search of food, and they found much difficulty in getting enough to eat. One day the mice met together to try and find a way out of their plight. 'I will tell you what to do,' said a young mouse. 'Let us tie a bell round the wretched cat's neck, then we can always hear her coming.'

On hearing this suggestion all the mice began to squeak with delight, except one old grey whiskered mouse who said, 'The advice is very good, but who will bell the cat?'

Now answer the following questions:

(a) Write down the conversation in this story.

(b) Where did the mice live?

(c) What feelings had the mice towards the cat?

(d) What did the young mouse suggest should be done to the cat?

(e) Why was this suggestion difficult to carry out?

6. Read the following:

Colby decided to go and see old Timmy Spragg, so he put on his hat and coat, much to his terrier's delight, and stepped out into the gloaming. Janet had warned him it was a difficult place to find, there were so many little twists and turns and by-roads. He walked through the village, past the church, whistling a gay little tune, and keeping an eye on his terrier frisking along the fence.

Presently the road dipped sharply down, and it grew darker. Colby saw a light or two winking redly from somewhere on his right, and guessed it was Spragg's cottage. Slipping a lead on Vixen, he pushed open the little gate and walked in. As he approached the door Timmy Spragg and a great hairy dog came around the corner of the cottage. Timmy swung an old-fashioned type of hurricane lamp in one hand and carried a basket of logs in the other. His great dog bounded angrily forward but was instantly checked.

'Good evening' said Colby. 'Are you Mr Spragg?' 'Yes' replied Timmy, suspiciously. 'I am told you are making some little stools and tables out of some very old oak.' 'That be right, sir,' agreed Timmy in a pleased voice. He was proud of his craftsmanship.

Old Spragg led the way into the cottage, which was spotlessly clean, from the red scrubbed bricks to the cheerful shining grate with its hissing logs and singing kettle. On a cupboard against the wall stood a case of stuffed birds, two corncrakes and an owl. Above the lintel of the door was another case containing a stuffed otter holding a grayling in his mouth. Over the rafters reposed two guns and on the mantelpiece stood a jar of feathers cut ready for pipe cleaning. 'Take a seat, sir,' invited Timmy. 'I'll fetch you one or two pieces to look at.' Colby sat down and looked around him. Timmy came back with a beautiful little stool the colour of very dark honey, 'Have a look at that 'un.' Colby did so admiringly. The workmanship was surprisingly good and the oak was sleek like the coat of a racehorse.

Read the above passage carefully and then answer the questions below:

(a) What time of day was it when Colby set out to find the cottage? Give reasons for your answer.

(b) Describe the way he went.

(c) Was Timmy's home easy to find? How did Colby discover it?

(d) What living things are mentioned in the passage? Say what you know about the dog.

(e) Describe the meeting of Colby and Timmy Spragg.

(f) What is said in the passage about the stool?

(g) Explain the following:

   (i) 'into the gloaming'

   (ii) 'the oak was sleek'

   (iii) 'frisking along'

   (iv) 'hurricane lamp'

   (v) 'craftsmanship'

   (vi) 'the lintel of the door'

(h) Use in sentences of your own the following words:

approached, reposed, checked, type, suspicious.

(i) Describe all that Colby could see in the cottage.

(j) Give one word that can be used instead of each of the following phrases:

   (i) over and over again

   (ii) in good time

   (iii) day in, day out

   (iv) one by one

   (v) little by little

7. Read the following:

I am quite big now. I am eight years old and my name is Ann. I go to school in England, but in the holidays I live at home as the other schoolgirls do. My home is on an island called Skokholm, in the Atlantic Ocean, not very far from the land of Wales.

One day when I had just come home from school to stay on the island, and was looking around me to see what I could play with, I came across the remains of the cook's galley from the wreck of the *Alice Williams*. It was lying beside one of the ruined buildings of the old farm, so I decided to make a house for myself out of it.

Now answer these questions in complete sentences:

(*a*) What is the name and the age of the girl in the piece?

(*b*) (i) Where does she live?

(ii) Where is her school?

(*c*) How did the *Alice Williams* come to be on the island?

(*d*) What was the condition of the old farm?

(*e*) What ocean touches the shore of Wales?

(*f*) What game did Ann play?

8. Read through the extract and then answer the questions:

Mr Winkle Goes Skating

All this time, Mr Winkle, with his face and hands blue with the cold, had been putting his skates on, with the points behind, and getting the straps into a very complicated and entangled state, with the assistance of Mr Snodgrass, who knew rather less about skates than a Hindoo. At length, however, with the assistance of Sam Weller, the unfortunate skates were firmly screwed and buckled on, and Mr Winkle was raised to his feet.

'Now, then, sir,' said Sam, in an encouraging tone; 'off with you, and show 'em how to do it.'

'Stop, Sam, stop!' said Mr Winkle, trembling violently, and clutching hold of Sam's arms with the grasp of a drowning man. 'How slippery it is, Sam!'

'Not an uncommon thing upon ice, sir,' replied Mr Weller, 'hold up, sir!'

This last observation of Mr Weller's bore reference to a demonstration Mr Winkle made at the instant of a frantic desire to throw his feet in the air, and dash the back of his head on the ice.

'These – these – are very awkward skates, ain't they, Sam?' inquired Mr Winkle, staggering.

'I'm afeered there's a orkard gen'l'm'n in 'em, sir,' replied Sam.

'Now, Winkle,' cried Mr Pickwick, quite unconscious that there was anything the matter. 'Come; the ladies are all anxiety.'

'Yes, yes,' replied Mr Winkle, with a ghastly smile, 'I'm coming.'

'Just a goin' to begin,' said Sam, endeavouring to disengage himself. 'Now, sir, start off!'

'Stop an instant, Sam,' gasped Mr Winkle, clinging most affectionately to Mr Weller. 'I find I've got a couple of coats at home that I don't want, Sam. You may have them, Sam.'

'Thankee, sir,' replied Mr Weller.

'Never mind touching your hat, Sam,' said Mr Winkle hastily. 'You needn't take your hand away to do that. I meant to have given you five shillings this morning for a Christmas-box, Sam. I'll give it you this afternoon, Sam.'

'You're wery good, sir,' replied Mr Weller.

'Just hold me at first, Sam; will you?' said Mr

Winkle. 'There – that's right. I shall soon get in the way of it, Sam . . . Not too fast, Sam; not too fast.'

(a) Copy out five sentences or phrases which show that Mr Winkle was not used to skating.

(b) The author says that Mr Snodgrass knew 'rather less about skates than a Hindoo.' Why a Hindoo?

(c) Why was Mr Winkle so kind to Sam, promising to give him five shillings and offering him two coats?

(d) Write out in correct English Sam's remarks which are underlined.

(e) Write another four or five lines to describe what you imagine happens to Mr Winkle when Sam lets go.

9. Read this passage very carefully:

The grim-looking stranger, having managed to answer the many searching questions of the guard, was at last left alone. Wearily he opened the window, letting in the welcome cooling breeze from the sea. Far below the bugles sounded the last calls of the day. He threw his belt and scabbard on the narrow bed and drew off his long spurred boots. Removing the wig which had so changed his appearance, he wiped the sweat and die from his face.

From his saddle-bag he took the precious box, the possession of which had already sent one man to a watery grave. The lock was almost eaten away by the sea-water in which it had lain, but the papers inside were still readable. In a moment he realised that his uncle's disappearance was planned for the day of his coronation. He had only four days in which to save the King!

Now answer the following questions in your own words:

(*a*) What did the stranger do when he was left alone?

(*b*) What could the stranger see from his window?

(*c*) What time of day was it?

(*d*) What was in the saddle-bag?

(*e*) How was the stranger disguised?

(*f*) How had the stranger travelled?

(*g*) What had happened to the previous owner of the box?

(*h*) Where had the box been hidden?

(*i*) Who was the stranger's uncle?

10. Read the following passage carefully:

One day when Rusty, Hazel and I were sitting in our nest, mother suddenly gave a low note of warning. Presently we heard footfalls down below, rustling in the dry pine-needles. The footsteps stopped just below our tree.

All at once a great jagged stone came crashing up within a yard of our home, frightening us all greatly. Mother crouched with us closer than ever in our frail little house of sticks, which was not made to stand the force of stones. Almost immediately another mass of whizzing stone fell even nearer than the first. This frightened Hazel so much that she jumped completely out of the nest. But mother was after her quick as lightning, and saved her from tumbling right down to the ground and being killed. The quick eyes of our enemies, however, had caught a glimpse of red fur in the pale green foliage.

After a few minutes' argument, it was decided that one of them should do the climbing. Presently I heard a bough creak, and then followed a scraping and grinding as his heavy hob-nailed boots clawed the trunk in an effort to reach the first branch. On he came. Soon he was only three or four branches below us.

Suddenly the fellow's great rough head was pushed up through the branches just below. None of us could move. Then up came a large dirty paw and grasped the very branch on which we lived. This was too much for mother. She made a sudden dash out of the nest and went straight for that grasping fist. Next instant her teeth met deep in the fellow's first finger. He gave one yell and let go. Luckily for himself, he fell upon a wide-spreading bough not far below, caught hold of it, and so saved himself from a tumble right down to the ground.

Now answer these questions:

(*a*) How many squirrels were in the nest?

(*b*) When did the mother squirrel give a note of warning?

(*c*) How did the enemies first attack?

(*d*) What did the squirrels do?

(*e*) What was the nest made of and what kind of tree was it in?

(*f*) Why did the mother squirrel leave the nest?

(*g*) How did the squirrels know that someone was trying to reach them?

(*h*) How was the enemy beaten back?

(*i*) What happened in the end to the climber?

(*j*) Where in the passage did you first guess that the story-teller is a squirrel?

11. Read this passage carefully and answer the questions below in your own words:

> On that day I was sitting in my room a little before supper, when John Paul burst open the door with no civility of knocking, and told me there was one below that wished to speak with the steward; sneering at the name of my office.
>
> I asked what manner of man, and what his name was; and this disclosed the excuse of John's ill-humour, for it appeared the visitor refused to name himself except to me, a sore affront to John Paul's self-esteem.
>
> 'Well,' I said, smiling a little, 'I will see what he wants.'
>
> I found in the entrance hall a big man, very plainly habited, and wrapped in a sea-cloak, like one new landed, as indeed he was. Not far off Macconochie was standing, with his tongue out of his mouth and his hand upon his chin, like a dull fellow thinking hard; and the stranger, who had brought his cloak about his face, appeared uneasy. He had no sooner seen me coming than he went to meet me with an effusive manner.

(a) What was the job of the man telling the story?

(b) Where had the visitor come from?

(c) What made John Paul in such an ill humour?

(d) In what way was the visitor's behaviour unusual?

(e) How do we know that the visitor was not expected?

(f) Explain in your own words the meaning of:

    (i) 'with no civility of knocking'

    (ii) 'sneering at the name of my office'

    (iii) 'a sore affront'

    (iv) 'an effusive manner'

12. Read carefully through the following poem and answer the questions at the end:

> Within a thick and spreading hawthorn bush,
> That overhung a molehill large and round,
> I heard from morn to morn a merry thrush
> Sing hymns to sunrise, and I drank the sound
> With joy; and, often an intruding guest,
> I watched her secret toils from day to day, –
> How true she warped the moss to form a nest,
> And modelled it within with wood and clay;
> And by and by, like heath-bells gilt with dew,
> There lay her shining eggs, as bright as flowers,
> Ink-spotted-over, shells of greeny blue;
> And there I witnessed, in the sunny hours,
> A brood of Nature's minstrels chirp and fly,
> Glad as that sunshine and the laughing sky.

(a) Where did the thrush build her nest?

(b) How was the nest made?

(c) What does the poet mean when he says:

'. . . and, often an intruding guest,

I watched her secret toils from day to day'?

(d) Write down the line of the poem that best describes the appearance of the thrush's eggs.

(e) What lines from the poem suggest that the eggs hatched and the young birds came out?

(f) Explain the meaning of the words underlined in the poem.

13. Read this carefully so that you can answer the questions:

> The chief outdoor amusements of the Normans were hunting, hawking, archery, bull-baiting, but the greatest sport was the tournament.

In those days every man of rank was a knight. He had to pass through a long course of training in the use of weapons, as almost everything was decided by combat. He had also to pledge himself to be loyal to the king, to defend religion, and to protect any lady in danger. Fighting was considered of more importance than learning, because men had so often to fight for their lands, and even for their lives.

When a knight went to battle he was clad from head to foot in armour. His shirt of mail was made of rings, and his helmet was shaped like a cone. On his shield a coat-of-arms was painted. His chief weapons were a lance, a two-handled sword, and a small dagger.

The tournament was a mock fight between two or more knights on horseback. The place of combat was a large open space, which was enclosed, and called the lists. Ladies and nobles sat in raised galleries to watch the trials of skill in the use of arms, and the 'Queen of Beauty' sat high above all on a throne. The weapons usually employed were lances without heads, but sometimes an unfortunate knight was wounded or unhorsed, and even killed. When the fight was over, the successful knight received a prize from the 'Queen of Beauty', who presided over the sports of the day.

(a) From reading the above passage, and *using your own words*, write a short description of a tournament, as if you yourself had been a looker-on.

(b) Why in Norman times was skill in arms more thought of than learning? What effect do you think this preference would have upon the life of the people?

(c) Describe briefly the duties of a knight.

(d) The following words occur in the passage: archery, loyal, coat-of-arms, enclosed, presided. Compose five sentences *of your own*, each including one of the above words to show you understand their meanings. Do not merely copy or slightly alter the sentences in which they occur. Write *new* sentences.

14. Read the following passage carefully:

He led the way into the next room, and down the stairs to the water. The tide was pretty full, so that I could dive off one ledge and climb out by the ledge on the other side. So I dived in and then climbed back, and dried myself with a piece of our old sail, feeling wonderfully refreshed. Then we went upstairs to the cave again, and supped off the remains of the dinner; and then the men sat about the table talking, telling each other stories of the sea. It was dusk before we finished supper, and the caves were dark, but no lights were allowed. The smugglers always went into the passages to light their pipes. I don't know how they managed in the winter; probably they lived in the passages, where a fire could not be seen from the sea. In summer they could manage very well.

Now answer these questions:

(a) Do you think the sea would ever enter the cave? Quote two phrases, which explain your answer.

(b) Why did the smugglers leave the cave to light their pipes after nightfall?

(c) Why does the writer think the smugglers 'could manage very well' in summer?

(d) Explain in your own words (one sentence for each answer):

    (i) 'The tide was pretty full'

    (ii) 'They supped off the remains of the dinner'

    (iii) 'Smugglers'

15. Read this passage very carefully:

> Round the corner came a small group of men whispering excitedly among themselves. I heard the words 'explosion,' 'collapse,' 'like rats in a trap,' 'shaft,' 'flooding,' 'gas.' The men were grimy and exhausted, their clothing was soiled and sodden, soaked through with rain and perspiration. They had just staggered wearily away from the colliery, in unwilling obedience to orders, after having slaved for more than forty-eight hours, in a vain attempt to tunnel through to their imprisoned mates.

Now complete each of the following sentences by using the correct word or phrase from the bracket at the end:

(a) The men were (soldiers; engineers; miners).

(b) They were excited about (a pit disaster; a forest fire; a railway collision).

(c) The men were (fresh and tidy; neat but dusty; wet and tired).

(d) They had worked (a whole day; over two days and nights; a half-day).

(e) The men were (glad to finish their work; eager to continue their work; anxious to start work).

(f) They were (marching along; running excitedly; hardly able to walk).

16. Read the following passage very carefully and then answer the questions which follow:

> One day towards the end of the year, when rain had been falling steadily since daybreak, so that water poured unceasingly from the gutter-pipes, and the *troughs* in the yard were flooded, Dick and his sister Annie heard a *commotion* outside while they were having tea.

About this time the ducks usually marched off to their pen, one behind the other, with their toes out, like soldiers drilling, but now they started to make a terrible quacking.

The two children ran out to see what the cause of it all might be. The ducks were pushing their gold-coloured bills here and there, and jumping on *the triangles of their feet*. Dick knew by the way they were *carrying on* that there must be something wrong in the duck-world, but Annie, who was quicker than Dick, started to count them, and when she made the total thirteen, she guessed what the trouble might be.

The children began to search about, the ducks running to lead them aright, and when they came to the end of the yard they found good reason for the distress of the birds. The old white drake, a bird of good manners and a loving father, always the last to help himself from the pan of barley-meal, and the first to show fight to a dog or a cock interfering with his family, was quacking vigorously, and he was evidently badly upset. For the brook, wherein he was accustomed to *dabble* and to search for tadpoles and caddis-worms, was now coming down in a great brown flood. The foam, the noise, and the up and down movement of the water, like waves upon the sea, were enough to frighten any duck, even one that had been brought up on stormy waters, and our ducks had certainly not been.

(a) What time of day was it?

(b) What season of the year was it?

(c) Why did the ducks remind the writer of soldiers drilling?

(d) Why were the ducks in the yard making a terrible quacking?

(e) Explain the meaning of the phrase 'the triangles of their feet.'

(f) What do you think Annie guessed the trouble might be after she had counted the ducks?

(g) What helped the children to find out where the cause of the trouble was?

(h) What example does the writer give to show:

(i) that the drake was a bird of good manners?

(ii) that the drake was a loving father?

(i) For what purpose do you think the drake had gone down to the brook?

(j) Why was the drake upset?

(k) What had caused the change in the brook?

(l) What is the meaning of each of the following words or phrases used in this passage?

(i) troughs

(ii) commotion

(iii) carrying on

(iv) dabble

17. Read the following passage carefully:

The Squirrel

Of all quadrupeds there is none so beautiful, so happy, so wonderful, as the squirrel. Innocent in all his ways, harmless in his food, playful as a kitten, but without cruelty, and surpassing the fantastic dexterity of the monkey, with the grace and brightness of a bird, the little dark-eyed miracle of the forest glances from branch to branch more like a sunbeam than a living creature: it leaps, and darts, and twines where it will; a chamois is slow to it; and a panther clumsy: grotesque as a gnome, gentle as a fairy, it haunts you, listens for you, hides from you, looks for you, loves you, as if the angel that walks with your children had made it himself for their heavenly plaything.

Now answer the following questions:

(a) Name all the *animals* mentioned in the passage.

(b) Write down all the words, (adjectives) which *describe the squirrel*.

(c) Name any other beings mentioned in the passage.

(d) Why does the writer call it '*the miracle of the forest*'?

(e) Do you consider the writer of this passage a good writer? Gives reasons for your answer.

18. Substitute one word for each of the phrases underlined in the following sentences:

(a) The <u>victorious kind</u> rode in triumph through the town.

(b) The letter is <u>so badly written</u> that it cannot be read.

(c) The boy has always been <u>very fond of hard work</u>.

(d) The burglar entered the room <u>making no noise</u>.

(e) The prisoner was declared <u>free from guilt</u>.

(f) I am glad the children are <u>enjoying good health</u>.

(g) The girl's work is <u>getting better</u> every day.

(h) As night fell, the noise and bustle of the city <u>grew less and less</u>.

(i) Tommy was an attractive little boy, but very <u>full of mischief</u>.

(j) His <u>large collection of books</u> was his most treasured possession.

19. Write what you know about any five of the following (not more than four lines on each):

Lewis Carroll	Shylock	Sherlock Holmes
Scrooge	Peter Pan	Hiawatha

GENERAL INTELLIGENCE/ KNOWLEDGE

1. Copy down the word at the beginning of each line. Then choose one word from the line that has the *opposite* meaning to the word in capital letters. Write it down.

    NEAR: close, remote, distance, open.

    LIKENESS: enemy, similar, enjoy, difference.

    ENLARGE: decrease, wider, picture, big.

    LOOSE: find, tight, escape, prisoner.

    ARRANGE: fix, grate, disturb, target.

    BEGIN: finish, start, conclusion, commence.

    AFTER: following, morning, behind, before.

    YOUNG: adult, father, aged, grow.

    LATE: time, punctual, hour, sooner.

    FOOT: hand, yard, summit, kick.

2. My best friend is tall and dark. I am nine and he is ten. He is one of these four boys below. Read the following sentences and write down my best friend's name.

    Harry is younger than me. He is short and dark.
    Dick is ten. He is a tall boy with fair hair.
    Tom has dark hair. He is older than me and is a tall boy.
    Frank is a tall boy with dark hair. He is nine.

3. One number in each line does not fit in properly with the others. Find this number and write it down.

    (a) 2, 5, 8, 11, 15, 17

    (b) 29, 26, 21, 17, 13, 9

    (c) 1, 9, 16, 23, 27, 31, 34

    (d) 2, 6, 18, 52, 162

   (*e*) 144, 120, 96, 75, 48, 24

   (*f*) 21, 19, 16, 13, 10

   (*g*) 1, 4, 16, 60

   (*h*) 4, 9, 14, 18, 24, 29

4. The letters A B C E H R S T X are to be put in the squares, *one* letter in each square, so that:

C and T are in the top row;

E and R are in the bottom row;

T and S are in the left-hand column;

R and X are in the right-hand column.

Fill in the squares with the proper letters.

5. Each of the sentences given here can be made into better sense by interchanging two words. Draw lines under those words.

Example: <u>Eggs</u> lay <u>hens</u>

Now do the sentences below for yourself. Remember, underline just two words in each sentence.

   (*a*) The path ran down the boy.

   (*b*) Jane bird like a flew.

   (*c*) The swam fish in the sea.

   (*d*) The dog down the cat chased the street.

   (*e*) The writing was teacher on the blackboard.

   (*f*) Jimmie sleeping the stroked cat.

   (*g*) Mother scrub Mary to told the floor.

   (*h*) There were many streets on the people.

   (*i*) Willie had ten or eleven birthday on his letters.

(*j*) They lay on the birds while the grass flew above them.

(*k*) The children were long after their hungry walk.

(*l*) John ran in the cake while James ate race in the refreshment room.

(*m*) Leaves were trees from the falling.

(*n*) The child while slept the wind blew.

(*o*) John wrote his book on his new name.

(*p*) My cousin is fortnight to stay with me in a coming.

(*q*) As their mother had a noise they were told not to make a headache.

(*r*) He read on his glasses and put a book.

(*s*) John was last of his class top year.

(*t*) As it was quietly heavily they had to play raining indoors.

(*u*) The frightened child man away from the angry ran.

(*v*) The squirrel top up to the climbed of the tree.

(*w*) Mabel singing round the garden ran at the top of her voice.

(*x*) Play school the children went to after.

(*y*) He gets eight when the clock strikes up.

(*z*) The sock was knitting a mother for her son.

6. (*a*) Write down words which describe a collection of: cows, fish, bees, sheep, crows.

   (*b*) What do the following letters stand for?

   U.S.A., B.B.C., H.M.S., P.T.O., U.N.O., H.R.H., M.P.

7. The leader of a Guide patrol is named Mary Jenkins;

so her surname is Jenkins, her Christian name is Mary, and her initials are M.J. There are 6 other girls in her patrol; each has 2 initials.

Surnames: Brown, Smith, Evans, Clark, Jones.

Christian names: Molly, Celia, Gwen, Ruth, Sally.

Two girls have surname and Christian names beginning with the same letter; two others are named Ruth. One of the twins has the same initials as the leader, and the other has the same Christian name as Evans.

Write down each girl's full name.

8. Look at this example:

cow, pig, horse, <u>grass</u>

Three of the words are names of animals. The other word is the name of a plant. It has been underlined because it is different from the others. Now go through the following examples, underlining the word in each row that you think is different from the other three.

(*a*) pencil, chalk, ruler, pen.

(*b*) velvet, muslin, calico, thread.

(*c*) yellow, green, red, colour.

(*d*) river, lake, sea, mountain.

(*e*) writing, book, story, novel

(*f*) milk, drink, water, tea

(*g*) book, volume, magazine, print

(*h*) carpet, rug, mat, mattress

(*i*) skate, stand, slide, slip

(*j*) cold, warm, heat, freezing

(*k*) policeman, soldier, sailor, airman

(*l*) round, shape, square, oblong

(*m*) shout, think, speak, whisper

(*n*) oak, ash, elm, palm

(*o*) sweet, rich, chocolate, sugary

(*p*) pen, pencil, paper, crayon

(*q*) hammer, plank, chisel, hatchet

(*r*) hat, cap, bonnet, scarf

9. Cross out clearly what is not wanted in this silly sentence, so that it shall read properly. Do not cross out too much, and do not add anything:

Until you are often told to let him go your end of the missing rope, hold it firmly in the left with hand.

10. Complete each of these sentences by underlining the right word in the bracket:

(*a*) BACK is to FRONT as HEEL is to (SIDE, TOE, PLACE).

(*b*) INK is to PEN as (HAIR, HANDLE, PAINT) is to BRUSH

(*c*) MAN is to CROWD as DROP is to (FALL, FLOCK, WATER).

(*d*) NOTE is to MUSIC as (SENSE, LENGTH, WORD) is to SENTENCE.

(*e*) HOUSE is to MAN as (SHELTER, HOME, HOLE) is to FOX.

11. One word in each group of four means the same or nearly the same as the word in capitals. Write this word down.

    Example: SMALL: baby, size, little, mouse

    Answer: little

    (a) CUT: knife, sever, canal, wound.

    (b) TWIN: engine, triplet, brother, duplicate.

    (c) OFTEN: sometimes, frequently, always, again.

    (d) POWER: might, strong, cable, electricity.

    (e) CLOTHES: washing, shut, frock, apparel.

12. Look at these particulars:

9 years old	Jim	Eric	
10 years old	Susan	Tom	
11 years old	Peter	Carol	Molly
Fair	Susan	Molly	Peter
Tall	Eric	David	Tom
No brothers or sisters	Molly	Peter	David
Good at English	Susan	Eric	Molly
Good at Arithmetic	David	Tom	Peter

    Now write:

    (a) The name of the boy who is a twin, tall, and will be eleven next year. He is good at arithmetic.

    (b) The name of the fair girl who is eleven years old. She is an only child and is good at English.

    (c) The name of the boy who is tall and good at arithmetic. He is a year younger than his sister, Susan.

13. For each sentence underlined, find the best reason among the four given. Then write down its number, (i), (ii), (iii) or (iv).

   (a) A clock is useful in the house.
      (i) We should be late for school without it.
      (ii) It often needs winding.
      (iii) It tells us the correct time.
      (iv) It gives a cheerful tick.

   (b) A tap should not be left running.
      (i) It will soon wear out.
      (ii) It wastes water.
      (iii) It makes an unpleasant noise.
      (iv) It is very careless.

   (c) Summer is a good time for swimming.
      (i) The sun is often shining.
      (ii) Most people have their holidays then.
      (iii) It is less likely to rain.
      (iv) The water is warm and pleasant.

14. Write down the word that you think will finish each line best.

   (a) Duke is to duchess as prince is to ....

   (b) Sheep is to mutton as pig is to ....

   (c) Light is to dark as heat is to ....

   (d) June is to May as September is to ....

   (e) Tar is to rat as part is to ....

   (f) Three is to six as four is to ....

15. The letters ERBDA are just the letters of the word BREAD mixed up. Now, straighten up the following:

   (a) AAANNB is a fruit which comes from abroad.

   (b) ROIIES is a large animal.

   (c) GRATEAMR is a girl's name.

   (d) DWEBORRA is an article of furniture.

   (e) SAIRINS are used in Christmas puddings.

16. Look at these carefully, and put in the figures left out in *five* of these rows:

   (a) 2, 3, 4, 5, 6, 7, 8, 9

   (b) 2, 4, 6, 8, ..., 12, 14, ...

   (c) ½, 1, 2, ..., ..., 16, 32, 64

   (d) 10, 20, 30, 40, 50, 60, 70, 80

   (e) 5, ..., ..., ..., ..., ..., ..., 40

   (f) 2, 5, 9, 14, 20, ..., 35, ...

   (g) 4, 14, 40, 140, 400, ..., 4,000, ...

17. In each of the following examples find the word in the brackets which is like the first four words:

   (a) Cup, jug, saucer, plate (Coat, pup, spoon, slate).

   (b) Ear, mouth, nose, throat (Toe, arm, leg, eye).

   (c) Apple, pear, plum, strawberry (Carrot, cauliflower, raspberry, cabbage).

   (d) Tulip, rose, wallflower, daffodil (Crocus, onion, grass, leaves).

   (e) Scissors, pincers, pliers, tweezers (Nails, trousers, shears, hammer).

18. Read the following carefully, then rewrite it, filling in the missing words (*one* in each space):

Mrs Harris went to dinner with Mrs Carter, her only friend. It —(a)— to be John Carter's fifteenth birthday; he and his father —(b)— in the garden —(c)— an important matter. Joyce Carter, Mrs —(d)— 's granddaughter had become a probationer nurse —(e)— she was eighteen. Peter Carter, the —(f)— was at school.

During the —(g)—, which they —(h)— enjoyed, —(i)— Carter said, 'Well, I have —(j)— way to John at last. Flower and vegetable growing does not —(k)— him, so now he has —(l)— he is going to —(m)— as a mechanic. He is my eldest —(n)— and I wish he had been —(o)— to —(p)— in my footsteps. I have been a —(q)— all my life and I —(r)— it good, —(s)— work for those who like —(t)— life.'

19. Complete the following by giving words expressing sound and ending in 'ing':

e.g. the humming of telephone wires.

(a) the .... of leaves.

(b) the .... of anvils.

(c) the .... of brakes.

(d) the .... of stairs.

20. Each of the following sentences here can be made into better sense by interchanging *two* words. Rewrite the sentences correctly.

Example: Milk like cats – Cats like milk.

(a) Our black cat had a retriever with the fight next door.

(b) The sea went to the family for a swim.

(c) The shepherd whistled by the gate and stood to his dog.

(d) A was stung by Joan bee.

(e) Sailors have to climb able to be.

21. In each of the sets of words given below there is *one* word meaning something rather different from the other three. Find the different word in each line and write it down:

(a) alike, same, similar, somewhat.

(b) pigeon, duck, goose, swan.

(c) bus, conductor, passenger, driver.

(d) this, that, the, those.

(e) firm, rough, solid, hard.

(f) desk, book, cupboard, drawer.

(g) spade, earth, sand, gravel.

(h) pretty, nice, charm, lovely.

(i) justice, merciful, pitying, forgiving.

(j) tumbler, cup, mug, jug.

(k) fishing, rowing, climbing, swimming.

(l) scarlet, blue, red, pink.

(m) sewing, cotton, needle, calico.

22. In a test, Nan got two more marks than Jill and three marks less than Susan.

(a) Who got most marks?

(b) If Susan got fifteen marks, how many did Jill get?

23. Write down the word that is missing from the end of each line.

   (a) *Shoe* is to *foot* as *glove* is to ....

   (b) *Nine* is to *three* as *fifteen* is to ....

   (c) *Hand* is to *finger* as *foot* is to ....

   (d) *Black* is to *white* as *tall* is to ....

   (e) *Cow* is to *herd* as *sheep* is to ....

   (f) *Day* is to *week* as *month* is to ....

   (g) *Quick* is to *fast* as *bitter* is to ....

   (h) *Milk* is to *bottle* as *jam* is to ....

   (i) *Apple* is to *fruit* as *kangaroo* is to ....

   (j) *Medicine* is to *chemist* as *flower* is to ....

24. The two words at the beginning of each line are related to one another. On each line, find another pair of words in the brackets that are related in the same way. Write down this pair.

   (a) chalk, blackboard (*book, paper, rubber, ruler, pencil*)

   (b) ring, finger (*neck, hand, bracelet, brooch, wrist*)

   (c) knee, leg (*elbow, bone, wrist, arm, shoulder*)

   (d) sister, brother (*cousin, niece, aunt, nephew, father*)

   (e) policeman, beat (*round, surgery, visit, medicine, doctor*)

   (f) green, grass (*red, lemon, yellow, snow, black*)

   (g) prince, princess (*queen, noble, duchess, lord, duke*)

   (h) mansion, house (*river, pond, stream, water, bridge*)

   (i) bed, bedroom (*table, nursery, chair, cot, mirror*)

   (j) actor, play (*theatre, concert, hall, film, musician*)

25. What *two* numbers should come next on each line? Write them down.

   (*a*) 1, 2, 4, 8, 16, 32, ..., ...

   (*b*) 1, 8, 15, 22, 29, 36, ..., ...

   (*c*) 63, 58, 53, 48, 43, 38, ..., ...

   (*d*) 2, 3, 5, 8, 12, 17, ..., ...

   (*e*) 8, 9, 7, 10, 6, 11, ..., ...

   (*f*) 3, 9, 27, 81, 243, ..., ...

   (*g*) 12, 9, 13, 8, 14, 7, ..., ...

   (*h*) 5, 8, 8, 12, 12, 17, ..., ...

26. Here is a simple code. Each letter stands for the letter above or below it.

   A   C   E   G   I   K   M   O   Q   S   U   W   Y
   B   D   F   H   J   L   N   P   R   T   V   X   Z

   So, GONE TO LUNCH = HPMF SP KVMDG

   What are these words written in code?

   ABQQFK, KFBTG, TRVJQF, DKFBM, SGQPMH.

   Write the answer to this question (your answer should not be in code):

   XGBS JT SGF CBSF PE APWJMH CBZ?

27. In your replies to this question write down numbers only.

   Example: (*a*) 2.

   (*a*) COME is the opposite of

      (1) HITHER   (2) GO   (3) APPROACH   (4) RUN

(*b*) Substract 29 from 41 and divide the result by 4.

(*c*) ORDINARY means the same as

(1) USEFUL   (2) PERMANENT   (3) ORDERLY
(4) USUAL

(*d*) WOOD is to DOOR as GLASS is to

(1) CUP   (2) WINDOW   (3) TABLE   (4) STEEL

(*e*) Which word is most unlike the others?

(1) LETTUCE   (2) ONION   (3) APPLE
(4) CABBAGE

(*f*) PARIS is a bigger city than VIENNA and VIENNA is bigger than ROME. Which is the smallest?

(1) PARIS   (2) VIENNA   (3) ROME

(*g*) DEAR is the opposite of

(1) POOR   (2) WASTEFUL   (3) CHEAP   (4) FREE

(*h*) One number in this row is wrong. Write the number which is wrong.

9, 7, 5, 2, 1

28. Read the information below:

1 roy = 15 ducas

1 duca = 6 floras

Now answer these questions:

(*a*) I buy an article worth 4 ducas. How much change should I receive out of 1 roy?

(*b*) I buy an article worth 2 roys 8 ducas and give the shopkeeper 3 roys. How much change should he give me?

(*c*) I buy 3 articles at 7 floras each. How much change should I receive out of 4 ducas?

29. Mr A, Mr B, Mr C and Mr D are four season-ticket holders travelling by the same train. Mr A's ticket allows him to get out at either Brasted, Westerham or Dunton Green; Mr B's ticket is for Knockholt or Dunton Green; Mr C's for Dunton Green or Sevenoaks; Mr D's for Brasted or Knockholt. No one gets out at either Sevenoaks or Westerham and only one person at Knockholt and one at Dunton Green.

(a) At what station does Mr A get out?

(b) At what station does Mr B get out?

(c) At what station does Mr C get out?

(d) At what station does Mr D get out?

30. Select and write down one of the answers below which makes the best answer to the following:

A woman who had fallen into the water was dragged out in a drowning condition by a man, but she did not thank him because:

(a) She never felt thankful for small things.

(b) She did not know the man well enough.

(c) She was feeling better.

(d) She was still unconscious.

ESSAYS AND COMPOSITIONS

1. Write a short account (about *four* or *five* lines) on any *four* of the following:
   - (*a*) Everest
   - (*b*) Westminster Abbey
   - (*c*) The Gothic
   - (*d*) Williams Shakespeare
   - (*e*) Queen Salote
   - (*f*) The Maoris

2. Imagine you are a scarecrow and tell a story about yourself.

3. Some children are playing at the seaside in an old boat – the tide rises – the boat floats out to sea – a thick fog comes down . . .

   Tell this story as vividly as you can, adding the excitement and fear of the parents, and finish the story in any way you like.

4. Write a composition on *one* of the following subjects:
   - (*a*) Imagine yourself on a long journey in an aeroplane. Your engine fails and you have to land on a desert island. Describe the island and tell what happens to you there.
   - (*b*) Write an account of an unfortunate picnic.
   - (*c*) Describe a market day in a country town.

5. Choose *one* of the following:
   - (*a*) Write a story ending with this sentence: 'Since that night I have not been out so late.'
   - (*b*) Write a story ending with these words: '. . . and that is why the old sailor was allowed to keep his parrot.'

(*c*) Write a story about a little dog, which begins with the words: 'Tim was very tired and was quite lost.'

(*d*) Finish the following story: 'It was now clear that I had lost my way. Moreover it had grown so dark that I could not read my map...'

6. Give an account of an imaginary talk between an eagle and an owl.

7. Imagine that you are an Englishman who lived a hundred years ago revisiting England today. Write about the changes you notice.

8. Imagine that the following is the beginning of a 'make-believe' story which you have started to write:

> One Saturday morning a little while ago, I had finished all my home duties before ten o'clock and found myself free for some hours, and, perhaps, even until bedtime. The weather gave promise of a fine day, all the more welcome because the rest of the week had been rather cold and wet. I was wondering how I could best spend my spare time and what I should ask permission to do, when, suddenly, there was a loud rat-tat at the front door.

Finish the story in your own words.

9. Write on one of the following subjects:

(*a*) A conversation between a policeman and a motorist he has stopped

(*b*) A letter to your parents while you are on holiday explaining that your money and return ticket have been stolen, and asking what you should do

(*c*) A newspaper paragraph of which the headline is 'Disappeared in a few minutes'

(*d*) The day I played for England

10. Give a short description of any *two* of the following:

    (*a*) A tractor

    (*b*) A telephone kiosk

    (*c*) A fire-engine

    (*d*) A fishing trawler

    (*e*) A baby's pram

11. Write an essay on *one* of the following subjects:

    (*a*) Description of 'The bravest deed that I know'

    (*b*) Camping

    (*c*) A school jaunt with one of the teachers

    (*d*) 'Gardening' or 'Sewing'

    (*e*) Eggs

    (*f*) Imagine yourself a cat and describe an interesting day in your life.

12. Write on any one of the following subjects:

    (*a*) The adventures of a library book

    (*b*) Suppose that a friend of yours who has been evacuated to Canada has asked for the latest happenings in the district in which you live. Write the letter in reply to your friend.

    (*c*) Tom and his sister Jane went for an hour's stroll with their dog, but the dog proved troublesome the whole time. Describe their experiences.

    (*d*) A visit to any one of the following: a fair, a circus, a market.

13. The following incidents occur in well-known books you may have read:

    (a) Tom comes down the wrong chimney.

    (b) Jim discovers the chart of Treasure Island.

    (c) Crusoe discovers a footprint in the sand.

    (d) Jo visits Laurie for the first time.

    (e) Alice drinks from the little bottle.

    (f) Black Beauty hears the hounds.

    Describe briefly two of these incidents.

14. Write a short essay of about *twenty* lines on *one* of the following subjects:

    (a) Imagine that you are a lion in a zoo, which is able to speak. What would you say about your life in the past and present to the people standing outside your cage?

    (b) One morning in school.

15. Choose *one* of the following:

    (a) Write a letter to a friend who has asked: 'What on earth do you do with yourself on a wet day in the holidays?'

    (b) Write a letter to a pen friend abroad, describing clearly your favourite game, the rules and how it is played.

    (c) A friend is coming to visit you who has never been to your house before. Write a letter giving the quickest route from the station to your house, being sure to mention all important landmarks.

    (d) Imagine you are staying with an aunt at her house by the river. Write a letter home to your parents telling them of your activities during the first week of your stay.

16. Which country in the world would you most like to visit? Explain why.

17. Write a composition on *one* of the following:

    (*a*) An ant's adventures in crossing a garden

    (*b*) A happy day

    (*c*) Sunset

18. Write a composition on *one* of the following subjects. Before starting the composition, you are advised to set down your scheme or plan and then keep the parts in separate paragraphs.

    (*a*) Kindness to birds and to animals

    (*b*) The happiest day I ever spent

    (*c*) A story about an elephant or a reindeer

    (*d*) A story of the adventure of a submarine or of a balloon

19. Write about twelve lines describing *one* of the following events. The description is begun for you – finish it:

    (*a*) A Ship in Distress
    Everybody in the neighbourhood was startled the other day, when it became known that a ship was sinking in . . .

    (*b*) Arrived in Time
    Last winter a large area of England was covered with deep snow. Many children were unable to . . .

    (*c*) Fun Day Out
    Last Monday the Sunday School children were taken for their annual outing to . . .

ANSWERS

ARITHMETIC

1. (*a*) 300
   (*b*) ⅚
   (*c*) 2.25

2. 506

3. 99 miles

4. £625

5. (*a*) 40 years old
   (*b*) 3 years' time
   (*c*) 30 years old

6. 4 hours 10 minutes

7. Monday

8. 2,765 books in 'A' section, 5,273 in 'B' section

9. 9,500 spectators

10. 1,500 seconds

EXAMINATION 2

1. 703,370
2. (a) 11; (b) 75
3. 105 minutes
4. 39 lettuce plants
5. 24 seconds
6. Albert had lost 7 marbles, Bob had won 4, Charles had lost 9 and Dan had won 12
7. (a) 4,832,100
   (b) 43
8. 84 bricks
9. 15 extra men
10. Fast by 7 minutes

EXAMINATION 3

1. 3,699
2. 105
3. (a) 7/20
   (b) 30 children
4. 790
5. 3 seconds per hour
6. 1.35 p.m.
7. 1/7 of her life
8. 16
9. 2.40 p.m.
10. £731

EXAMINATION 4

1. 165,742 and 82,871
2. (*a*) 37.2064
   (*b*) 3¹⁴⁄₃₉
3. 150
4. 357 words per page
5. 3.35 p.m.
6. 200 m.p.h.
7. 47 hours
8. 60 miles
9. 36 minutes
10. 14 boys

EXAMINATION 5

1. 76 minutes
2. 0.221
3. 36 days
4. 174 people
5. (*a*) 5.23 p.m.
   (*b*) 7.06 a.m.
   (*c*) 13 hrs 43 minutes
6. 9.36 a.m.
7. 11.29 a.m.
8. Monday
9. 0.65
10. 850

EXAMINATION 6

1. 751
2. 190
3. (a) 4,800 seconds
   (b) 12.05 p.m.
4. 3 *or* 10 trees
5. 153½ miles
6. £318.50
7. £400
8. 32 minutes
9. 96 miles
10. ⁵⁄₁₂

EXAMINATION 7

1. 7,809
2. 0.05
3. 60 miles
4. 102 miles
5. £22,500
6. 1.63 miles
7. 16 marbles
8. 40 miles
9. (a) 142,896
   (b) 738
10. 134 people

EXAMINATION 8

1. 204,009
      70,908
    450,070
    107,395
    ———
    832,382

2. (a) 509
   (b) 5.99

3. 5 ft 2 in.

4. 49 whole eggs

5. 8.36 a.m.

6. 324 children

7. (a) 16,000 voted
   (b) ⅝ voted
   (c) Jones by 1,278 votes

8. 42 marbles

9. One child has 35, the other 65

10. 1.35 p.m.

EXAMINATION 9

1. 12,012

2. (a) 21½
   (b) 18.02

3. 14 minutes

4. 48 sums

5. 1 hour 49 minutes

6. 10.35 a.m.

7. 5 teachers

8. 192 tins

9. 30

10. 2 minutes fast

EXAMINATION 10

1. (a) 990
   (b) 300
   (c) 205
   (d) 1.25
   (e) $\frac{1}{10}$

2. 506

3. 32 miles

4. 14 years 3 months

5. (a) Train 'A' arrives first
   (b) 36 minutes

6. 3.20 p.m.

7. 18,700 votes

8. Monday

9. 9⅝ hours *or* 9 hours 37½ minutes

10. 21:47.

EXAMINATION 11

1. (a) 470
   (b) 0.047
   (c) 4.2
   (d) 0.4

2. (a) D's share is 0.32 of the business
   (b) £3,200

3. 0.6

4. 33 miles

5. 21 years

6. 44 minutes

7. (a) 12.09 p.m.
   (b) 6 days

8. 407 miles

9. ¾

10. 5 less

EXAMINATION 12

1. (a) 4
   (b) 6⁷⁄₁₀
   (c) 1
   (d) 8
   (e) 48

2. 64

3. 105.1296

4. 4.05 p.m.

5. 10,066

6. 195 minutes

7. 451 minutes

8. 15 m.p.h.

9. 36 years old

10. Mary scored 60

EXAMINATION 13

1. (a) 76

   (b) 46

   (c) 4,019

   (d) 38,256,732

   (e) 1⅝

2. 6 hours 40 minutes

3. (a) 37

   (b) ⅜

   (c) 5

4. 1,790 eggs

5. 16 miles

6. 4¾ hours or 4 hours 45 minutes

7. 168 beads

8. 224 only

9. 56 boys stayed home

10. 5¼ hours

EXAMINATION 14

1. 3,494,784

2. 56 boys

3. (*a*) 15.271   (*b*) 228.78

4. 46 days

5. 11.15 a.m.

6. 12.13 p.m.

7. 100 more women

8. (*a*) $\frac{1}{10}$ (*b*) 0.006   (*c*) 16

9. Saturday

10. 30,200 people

EXAMINATION 15

1. (*a*) 10,705
   (*b*) 14,441
   (*c*) 1,913
   (*d*) 603

2. 29

3. 168

4. 36

5. 3 × 5 × 11

6. (*a*) 36
   (*b*) 2 × 3 × 5 × 7
   (*c*) 7, 5, 4

7. 13$\frac{5}{7}$ miles

8. (a) 27.32
   (b) 18.37
   (c) 9,003

9. 10.16 p.m.

10. 220 miles

GENERAL ENGLISH

EXAMINATION 1

1. (a) victory
   (b) cowardice
   (c) imports
   (d) death
   (e) sunrise
   (f) enemy
   (g) success
   (h) ascent

2. (a) Our cats caught mice.
   (b) Their grocers have no butter.
   (c) These knives are very blunt.
   (d) Women who live in shoes are sure to have troubles with their children.

3. Towards October, the bear came back. 'My friends down there wish me to present their compliments,' he said, and he picked some curious things out of his shaggy coat. 'Here, you shall see what I have for you.' 'What is it?' asked the oak. 'This is a beech nut,' answered the bear.

4. (a) toe
   (b) hive
   (c) Spaniards
   (d) length
   (e) referee
   (f) destruction
   (g) Dwarf
   (h) ugliness
   (i) Sorrow
   (j) depth

5. (a) My father bought me a green bicycle (or: My father bought me a bicycle, which was green).
   (b) I saw a red flower in your garden, which had a lovely scent.
   (c) We were not able to play football today because it was raining.
   (d) I could not walk along the narrow lane because the snow had drifted into it.

EXAMINATION 2

1. (a) Who's afraid of the big bad wolf?
   (b) Those books are the ones I want to read.
   (c) I took a parcel to their house.
   (d) The dog can see its master when it's standing by the gate.
   (e) She has forgotten where she put her knitting.

2. 'In the evening I always go for a walk. Sometimes I see nothing interesting, but sometimes I do see something worth describing. One night as I looked over the sea, I

noticed a strange light and there was a boat full of German sailors coming ashore. They were all very quiet, but I heard clearly the splash of their oars.'

3. (a) People who live in glass houses should not throw stones. This means do not be hypocritical.

   (b) A rolling stone gathers no moss. This means someone who is always on the move will never have roots or stability (often meant in the financial sense).

   (c) P.S. means postscript. This means 'after the main body of the text'.

   (d) A bird in the hand is worth two in the bush. This means you should appreciate what you have instead of chasing after more.

4. The boy *whom* we met at the baths and *who* spoke to *you* and *me* is Harry Baines; he *used* to live near me and he often *came* to my house to play with me. He had a good stamp collection; the total number of his stamps *was* more than three thousand. *He* and *I were* great friends.

5. (a) I was *certain* that the door was locked.

   (b) I shall finish reading this book *shortly*.

   (c) She *decided* to go shopping.

   (d) He drove his car to the *garage*.

   (e) He ran *quickly* to the station.

EXAMINATION 3

1. 'I saw Mrs Jones in the town this morning,' I said as I walked into the kitchen. 'Did you, dear?' said mother, 'And what did she say?' 'We didn't speak,' I replied, 'She was busy shopping and I was in a hurry to get home.'

2. (a) lived
   (b) ugly
   (c) cruel/unkind
   (d) like
   (e) them
   (f) foot
   (g) given
   (h) house
   (i) large/glamorous/royal/great
   (j) handsome
   (k) Both
   (l) going/invited
   (m) As
   (n) of
   (o) dress
   (p) been
   (q) Poor
   (r) gone/left
   (s) down
   (t) because

3. (a) He tripped his sister *unintentionally*
   (b) *Fearless*, he went alone into the haunted room.
   (c) The mother *mended* the frock.
   (d) The doctor saved the life of the *patient*
   (e) The captain *decided* to sail at dawn.

4. (a) The chair on which he stood was by the window.
   (b) I'd rather have/eat an apple than a pear.
   (c) The shortest of the twins was the strongest.

(*d*) It is difficult to share one small apple between six people.

(*e*) I asked him if his name was William.

5. (*a*) airport

(*b*) submarine

(*c*) thermometer

(*d*) zoo

(*e*) orchard

(*f*) artist

(*g*) choir

(*h*) tributary

(*i*) plumber

(*j*) jury

EXAMINATION 4

1.

62 Green Lane
Aytown

2 January, 1955

Dear Rose,

Thank you very much for your Christmas card and good wishes for the New Year. I hope you had a very jolly time, and that 1955 will be a very happy year for you. I am looking forward to seeing you in the summer.

Your loving friend,

Beryl

2. (*a*) dirty

(*b*) retreat

 (c) useless

 (d) dryness

 (e) impossible

 (f) strength

 (g) structured

 (h) forbid

 (i) presence

 (j) wisdom

3. (a) taught

 (b) saw

 (c) brought

 (d) held

 (e) cut

4. (a) near

 (b) old

 (c) swiftly/immediately/quickly

 (d) forgot

 (e) easily

5. Sam Weller took his hat and hastened to meet his father, who, on seeing his son approach, said, 'Well, I'm glad to see you, Sammy, and how are you this morning?'

EXAMINATION 5

1. (a) narrow

 (b) dim/dull

 (c) kind

 (d) inedible/uneatable

(e) invisible

(f) good

(g) slowly

(h) rough

(i) expensive

(j) sweet

2. (a) I waited until he had closed the door.

(b) I have helped him with his homework many times.

(c) I think the first day of the year is always exciting.

(d) He switched on the wireless and listened to the programme.

(e) She asked me to write a letter.

3. (a) sister

(b) niece

(c) nun

(d) witch

(e) goose

(f) mermaid

(g) waitress

(h) heroine

(i) vixen

(j) cousin

4. (a) The angry geese snapped at my bare feet.

(b) These young deer lived in yonder valleys.

(c) The police-constables chased the thieves across the roofs.

(d) He will come for you but not for us.

5. (a) The boy *decided* to sell his bicycle.

(b) The girl tried *repeatedly* until she succeeded.

(c) The vehicle was *immobile / stationary*.

(d) The soldier was forced to *surrender*.

(e) My brother always comes to school *punctually*.

(f) The soil is *barren*.

(g) The firm's books were examined *annually*.

(h) Some animals are *invisible* at night.

EXAMINATION 6

1. (a) John went from one bad situation to an even worse one.

   (b) He was caught committing a crime.

   (c) Make use of favourable conditions.

   (d) He sounds worse than he is.

   (e) The boy always has an answer.

   (f) His excuse wouldn't stand up to inspection.

2.   The evening is coming,
     The sun sinks to rest,
     The rooks are all flying
     Straight home to the nest.
     'Caw', says the rook,
     As he flies overhead,
     'It's time little people
     Were going to bed.'

3. beautiful, sloping, glassy, friendly, doubting, expensive, delightful, sleeping, dangerous, sporting/sporty

4. (a) A crate of apples has been hidden by the thieves.

(*b*) Each of the men wears a number on his shirt.

(*c*) I will be drowned and no one will save me.

(*d*) The largest of the two tigers sprang out of the cage.

(*e*) That is the boy about whom I have spoken to you.

5. It was such a *lovely* day that Jane and Peter decided to go for a *pleasant* walk. They had a *good* breakfast, and their mother gave each of them a *tasty* apple and a *delicious* piece of cake. Off they went up the hill to the woods, passing several *magnificent* houses on the way. From the top of the hill they had a *great* view of the countryside. Jane picked some *pretty* flowers, while Peter looked for birds' nests.

There are a number of different alternatives for this passage.

EXAMINATION 7

1. (*a*) It was a long day.

(*b*) I long for the day that I can drive.

(*c*) I want the cake.

(*d*) His want was greater than his need.

(*e*) I threw the ball up.

(*f*) It is a night owl.

(*g*) The haul yielded many fish.

(*h*) I heat the water until it is boiling.

2. Irregular, incapable, nonsense, illegal, unconcerned

3. (*a*) 'Hurry!' shouted John, 'the train is in.' 'We have another minute,' his friend replied.

(*b*) 'Is the honey good?' asked Mr Lion. 'It is delicious,' replied the jackal.

4.   But – conjunction
     the – definite article
     Giant – noun
     immediately – adverb
     put – verb
     them – pronoun
     into – preposition
     his – possessive pronoun
     gloomy – adjective
     dungeon – noun

5. (a) The Chairman stood up and made a lengthy speech.
  (b) The old man had reached the age of ninety-five.
  (c) The morning sun shone straight into his bedroom.
  (d) The girl had grown to her full height.
  (e) They saw the birds again in the evening.

EXAMINATION 8

1. I was passing by two boys who had found a nut when they asked me to decide whose it was. Both claimed it, one because he saw it first, the other because he picked it up. I cracked the nut and gave half the shell to each boy, telling them that I would take the kernel for myself as my fee for acting as judge.

   There are other possible solutions to this.

2. (a) My mother is in extremely good health.
  (b) I have not hidden the scissors: I placed them in the tin.
  (c) I would like to come and have tea with you on Wednesday, if that is alright with you.
  (d) George is sitting on the floor because he does not like sitting on chairs.

(e) The lady in the fur coat is the owner of the mansion on the hill, Mrs Thornton.

3. (a) boys; (b) eggs; (c) benches; (d) oxen; (e) boxes; (f) enemies; (g) hares; (h) hairs; (i) fish; (j) sheep

4. On the Arctic coasts of North America live the Eskimos. They exist mainly on seals and fish, which they catch in summer. Their hunting is done by means of boats called kayaks. These are made by stretching seal-skins over a light wooden frame. Because of their light weight, the boats are easily carried across the ice.

5. (a) accident; (b) hotel; (c) rumour; (d) acquaintance

EXAMINATION 9

1. 'Son, son,' said his mother, waving her tail. 'Now attend to me, and remember what I say. A hedgehog curls himself up into a ball and his prickles stick out every way at once. By this you may know the hedgehog. 'I don't like this old lady a bit,' said Stickly Prickly. 'I wonder what else she knows.' 'A tortoise can't curl himself up,' Mother Jaguar went on. 'By this you may know the tortoise.'

2. (a) course; (b) rink; (c) course; (d) court; (e) alley/green

3. (a) crawled, trudged, trotted, galloped, raced
   (b) whispered, murmured, rumbled, boomed, thundered

4. (a) swam; (b) I; (c) saw; (d) who; (e) was

5. (a) muddy boots; exciting adventure; careless mistake; bitter wind; brisk walk

There are many possible answers to part (b).

EXAMINATION 10

1. (a) sentry
   (b) diary
   (c) century
   (d) fascists
   (e) hospital
   (f) ambulance
   (g) widower
   (h) oasis
   (i) rehearsal
   (j) migrants

2. Verbs – enjoyed, sang, played, thought, danced, recited, acted, ended

   Adverbs – thoroughly, beautifully, well, gracefully, excellently, superbly, heartily

3. (a) The boys are flying their kites in the fields.
   (b) The ponies were in the same meadows as the oxen.
   (c) The girls' scarves were found in the boxes.
   (d) The trout lie motionless whilst their enemies watch them with great patience.

4. (a) A doctor diagnoses and prescribes treatment for people who are ill.
   (b) A cobbler makes and mends shoes.
   (c) An architect designs buildings.

5. Tom and Susan are two very *agreeable* children and their uncle, who is a *lovely* man, thought it would be *pleasant* to invite them to his farm. They spent a very *enjoyable* fortnight with him, and they would like a *splendid* holiday like this every year.

   There are many possible answers to this question.

EXAMINATION 11

1. (a) He was late for school this morning.
   (b) She turned right at the crossroads.
   (c) Take care not to blot your book.
   (d) Please help me to find my way.
   (e) Many people will be coming to the concert.

2. (a) animosity/no affection
   (b) in trouble
   (c) irritating
   (d) almost able to recall/beginning to remember
   (e) tired or near death

3. (a) He and his sister went to the pictures.
   (b) The girl said she had done it herself.
   (c) One of the thieves was caught.
   (d) Give me those oranges.
   (e) The man learned to swim.
   (f) The lady sings quite nicely.
   (g) He did not expect/accept the handsome present.
   (h) Neither one nor the other is correct.
   (i) I was so breathless I could hardly speak.
   (j) A kinder man never lived.

4. (a) reads – reeds
   (b) might – mite
   (c) fourth – forth
   (d) serf – surf
   (e) mail – male
   (f) wears – wares

(g) mussel – muscle

(h) waist – waste

5. (a) He was very interested in my story.

(b) His cap is a different colour from mine.

(c) She walked gaily across the road.

(d) Teacher was very pleased with my work.

(e) I seized him by the throat.

EXAMINATION 12

1. I think it is time for Bill to go home, and tell him so. Bill puts on his hat and coat, opens the door and runs down the path. When he comes to the gate, he stops for a moment and turns. Then he throws the ball back to me.
   'Here,' he says, 'you can keep this.'

2. (a) passed, his

   (b) may

   (c) Those, whose

   (d) His, were, too

   (e) two, past, their

3. Many different possibilities for answers, so long as they're sensible! e.g. (a) slabs of stone (b) glass (c) a blooming rose (d) the dead of night (e) in a peaceful dream

4. Mr and Mrs Smith have three children. The eldest is Susan, who is twelve. Last year, she passed her examination. Now, she has just started at a new school. She likes it very much and works hard. The other two are Peter and Doris. They are twins and are nine years old.

5. (a) 5; (b) 8; (c) 7; (d) 2; (e) 3; (f) 4; (g) 6; (h) 1

EXAMINATION 13

3. The swallow oft beneath my thatch
   Shall twitter from her clay-built nest.
   Oft shall the pilgrim lift the latch
   And share my meal, a welcome guest.
   Around my ivied porch shall spring
   Each fragrant flower that drinks the dew,
   And Lucy at her wheel shall sing
   In russet gown and apron blue.

2. (a) The shells, which I found on the shore, are pretty.

   (b) The policeman spoke to the man who was standing by the lamp-post.

   (c) Mr and Mrs Johnson are very pleasant people, whose son is my best friend.

   (d) I could not find the boy whom I was looking for.

   (e) Mrs White, whom I have known for many years, has gone abroad.

3. (a) taught

   (b) gone

   (c) flown

   (d) sewn

   (e) shot

   (f) rung

   (g) whom

   (h) whose

   (i) could, found

4. (a) Where is my dress?

   (b) Why did you leave?

   (c) Who is that strange man?

(d) When will you tidy your room?

(e) How long is the necklace?

5. (a) fare

(b) confident

(c) dye

(d) written

(e) loose

EXAMINATION 14

1. <u>Children</u> who go to the <u>library</u> must be <u>good</u>. If they are not, the <u>librarian</u> will send them out <u>immediately</u>. All <u>borrowers</u> must <u>return</u> the books within fourteen days or else they are <u>fined</u> one penny. Books must be kept <u>clean</u> when they are being read. Books can be borrowed only <u>under</u> these conditions.

2. (a) I asked if he had done his homework.

(b) I have torn my coat on a nail.

(c) He has fallen off the ladder and hurt himself.

(d) We went to the door but found she had gone.

(e) They ran away when I shouted to them.

3. 'How will you know your uncle's house?' Mary asked me. 'As far as I remember,' I replied, 'it's a white-green tiled house. I believe a house called The Willows is next door.'

4. (a) There is a cat on the lawn and I think it's ours.

(b) She lay on the bed for a rest.

(c) There were no other people in the field where we had our picnic.

    (*d*) Tom and Jim both write well, but Tom is the more careful of the two boys.

    (*e*) She had to practise on the piano every day.

5. (*a*) Each of you shouts loudly but neither of you speaks clearly.

    (*b*) Do Tom and his brother know that Mary and her mother were kept waiting?

    (*c*) Either the cat or the dog is sleeping, for neither the mouse nor the rat runs away.

    (*d*) We do not care to whom you give the presents so long as you do not give them to Bob and her.

    (*e*) Tell me the answer and I shall tell her.

    (*f*) After the mill-worker had woven the cloth, she found it had shrunk.

EXAMINATION 15

1. (*a*) flight
   (*b*) song
   (*c*) gift
   (*d*) thought
   (*e*) bearer/bearing

2. (*a*) from
   (*b*) woollen
   (*c*) Whom
   (*d*) affectionate
   (*e*) was
   (*f*) perennial
   (*g*) captain
   (*h*) injury

    (*i*) paralysed

    (*j*) avalanche

3. (*a*) Jim and I saw him do it.

    (*b*) None of my books is very exciting.

    (*c*) He has dropped the plate and broken it.

    (*d*) Mary and I did our homework together.

    (*e*) Where are those people going?

4. Her house is always full of cats.
   She has two cats, a dog and a parrot.

5. At four o'clock, Margaret and John turned the corner.
   They gazed with wonder. What had they seen? In front
   of their father's house stood a brand new car. 'What a
   beautiful car,' exclaimed John, who was jumping with
   joy.

EXAMINATION 16

1. (*a*) which

    (*b*) whom

    (*c*) whose

    (*d*) who

    (*e*) what

2. (*a*) sale, buy, consumption, imagination

    (*b*) prove, refuse, vary, provide

    (*c*) ragged, dreamy, perplexed, wasteful/wasted

    (*d*) mummies, men-of-war, curiosities, crockery

3. (*a*) 'I am going to the pictures,' said Sally.

    (*b*) 'My tooth is aching,' complained Tommy.

(c) 'Run for the doctor,' mother told me.

(d) 'You will have to wait for ten minutes,' remarked Mr Roberts.

(e) 'May I borrow your pencil?' asked Anne.

4. (a) too
   (b) chute
   (c) flower
   (d) pane
   (e) meet

5. (a) too
   (b) for
   (c) regarding, about
   (d) from
   (e) with
   (f) whom
   (g) than
   (h) by
   (i) so
   (j) with
   (k) from
   (l) between
   (m) whose
   (n) was
   (o) over, about

EXAMINATION 17

1. (a) modest; (b) sarcastic; (c) ungrateful; (d) polite;
   (e) ravenous

2. (a) On the table were two long pipes.
   (b) I was tired, so I lay down.
   (c) He is as good as she.
   (d) The river doesn't run uphill.
   (e) Neither Holland nor France is rich in minerals.
   (f) The cat as well as the dog is white.
   (g) The good temper of the children charms me.
   (h) I suffer more from the quarrel than he.
   (i) Within the cell stand two cloaked figures.
   (j) He has just written to his father.

3. (a) pocket money
   (b) change
   (c) fare
   (d) savings
   (e) wage

4. When I listen to the squirrel twittering away to the air, I realise that spring and higher temperatures are coming. (Or similar.)

5. (a) pleasant; mounted; reached; visited; delicious; refreshing; returned; tasty; restful
   (b)   (i) from
       (ii) drop
      (iii) visible
      (iv) gaze
       (v) situation

EXAMINATION 18

1. (a) 'Where are you going?' he asked me.
   (b) 'I am going to the station,' I replied.
   (c) 'I have lost your money,' she told my mother.
   (d) 'The tea is cold,' he complained.

2. (a) This is not an Infants' School.
   (b) I am told that Tom Jones's brother has won a scholarship.
   (c) The bishop and another gentleman then entered the hall.
   (d) When the dog recognised me it wagged its tail..
   (e) The matter does not concern you or me.
   (f) While talking to my friend, the bus passed me.

3. (a) The monkeys play on the branches of the trees.
   (b) The ladies have sliced the loaves and are peeling potatoes.
   (c) They have put their scarves on.
   (d) The old men sit on benches in the shade.
   (e) They have taken the geese to the ponds.

4. (a) scent
   (b) grate
   (c) herd
   (d) sale
   (e) bare

5. The grass-cutter moves to and fro across the open expanse of land, chopping the tall verdant turf and the heliotrope trefoil. (Or a similar re-wording.)

COMPREHENSION

1. (*a*) Edward was fourteen when he started work with Lawyer Ford, and had been in the job for thirty-five years.

   (*b*) This period seemed endless to Edward because he was working with only one other person so did not have people to talk to; he earned a low wage; the room he sat in was 'grimy'; his work was repetitive/monotonous.

   (*c*) You know Edward lived before the present day because of the of the references to 'shillings' and 'half a crown'.

   (*d*) People think Edward is 'a decent fellow, a confirmed bachelor, an excellent clerk and a thrifty individual'.

   (*e*) Edward was not married. We know this because he is described as 'a confirmed bachelor'.

   (*f*) (i) Stunted means not full-grown

   (ii) Furtively means secretly

   (iii) The indispensable lad means the vital or necessary young man

   (iv) A thrifty individual means someone who is careful with their money

2. (*a*) Robin Hood was brought up on the edge of Sherwood Forest, in the county of Nottingham.

   (*b*) Robin's life was changed when his father's enemies attacked their home and killed his father.

   (*c*) He 'barely escaped with his life' means that either he was badly injured nearly to the point of death, or was very nearly killed by someone but escaped.

   (*d*) After his home had been burnt, Robin fled into the depths of Sherwood Forest.

(e) 'He would feed on the King's deer' means that he caught and ate the deer in Sherwood Forest, which belonged to the King.

(f) Robin Hood was an outlaw.

3. (a) The Fox lied about the Crow having white feathers and a beautiful voice.

(b) The Fox got the cheese by persuading the Crow to sing, which made it open its beak and drop the cheese.

(c) The cheese came from a cottage window.

(d) The credulity of the Crow means that the Crow is easily fooled by lies.

(e) The lesson we are expected to learn from this story is not to be fooled by flattery.

4. (a) Two queer things that Father William did were to stand on his head and turn a back-somersault in at the door.

(b) Father Williams changed his mind because he is sure he doesn't have a brain to injure.

(c) 'Incessantly' means repeatedly, without relief. A back-somersault is when someone jumps over backwards.

(d) The word 'supple' means flexible. Father Williams kept supple by using an ointment.

(e) The signs of old age Father Williams showed were white hair and growing fat.

5. (a) 'I will tell you what to do,' said a young mouse. 'Let us tie a bell round the wretched cat's neck, then we can always hear her coming.'
    'The advice is very good,' replied one old grey whiskered mouse, 'but who will bell the cat?'

(b) The mice lived in the cellar of a lofty house.

(c) The mice had feelings of enmity and fear towards the cat.

(d) The young mouse suggested that the cat have a bell tied round its neck so they could hear it coming.

(e) This suggestion was difficult to carry out because the cat would have tried to eat any mouse that attempted to put the bell on its neck.

6. (a) It was dusk when Colby set out to find the cottage. We know this because the writer refers to him stepping out 'into the gloaming', which means dusk; the phrase 'it grew darker' shows the daylight is disappearing; and the writer refers to Colby following 'a light or two winking redly', which he would not see in the day time.

(b) Colby went through the village, past the church, down a road that dipped sharply and turned right to Spragg's cottage.

(c) Timmy's home was difficult to find, as Janet had warned Colby. Colby discovered it by following the twists and turns that Janet had mentioned and then by guessing that the red lights that he saw to his right would be Spragg's cottage.

(d) The living things mentioned in the passage are: Colby, Janet, Timmy Spragg, Vixen the terrier, and Timmy's great hairy dog. Colby's dog is called Vixen, loves going for walks, and runs along fences.

(e) Timmy Spragg is wary of Colby at first, but then is pleased when Colby enquires about his furniture making, and welcomes him into his cottage. Once they are inside Timmy fetches a couple of pieces made of oak for Colby to look at. Colby is very impressed by them.

(f) The stool is described as being the colour of 'very dark honey', of surprisingly good workmanship, and made of oak that was 'sleek like the coat of a racehorse.'

(g) (i) 'Into the gloaming' means he stepped out in the evening.

(ii) 'The oak was sleek' means glossy, in this case probably polished.

(iii) 'Frisking along' means bounding playfully along.

(iv) A 'hurricane lamp' is a type of lamp designed to withstand hurricanes.

(v) 'Craftsmanship' refers to the manual skill put into making the furniture.

(vi) 'The lintel of the door' is the beam-like structure placed over an entrance way.

(h) Many possible answers, e.g. 'I approached the stranger to ask the time.'
'The lady reposed at leisure in the afternoon.' 'The man checked his pockets.' 'What type of animal is it?' 'I was suspicious at first, but now I trust them.'

(i) Colby could see a clean house, with red scrubbed bricks; a shining grate with logs in it; a kettle; a cupboard against the wall with a case on it containing two stuffed corncrakes and a stuffed owl. He could also see the lintel above the door with another case above it containing a stuffed otter with a grayling in its mouth; two guns above the rafters; a jar of feathers on the mantelpiece; and the furniture that Timmy brought him.

(j) (i) repeatedly

(ii) promptly/quickly

(iii) daily

(iv) individually

(v) gradually

7. (a) The girl is called Ann and she is eight years old.

   (b) (i) She lives in England during school terms and on Skokholm island in the Atlantic Ocean during the holidays.

      (ii) Her school is in England.

   (c) The *Alice Williams* came to be on the island because it was wrecked on its shores.

   (d) The old farm was in ruins.

   (e) The Atlantic Ocean touches the shore of Wales.

   (f) Ann decided to play a game of making a house.

8. (a) 'putting his skates on, with the points behind, and getting the straps into a very complicated and entangled state'
'with the assistance of Mr Snodgrass, who knew rather less about skates than a Hindoo'
'the unfortunate skates'
'Mr Winkle, trembling violently, and clutching hold of Sam's arms with the grasp of a drowning man'
'a frantic desire to throw his feet in the air, and dash the back of his head on the ice'
'inquired Mr Winkle, staggering'
'I'm afreered there's an orkard gen'l'm'n in 'em, sir'

   (b) The author says a Hindoo because they come from India and therefore are unused to freezing temperatures and skating.

   (c) Mr Winkle was so kind to Sam because he did not want him to let go of his arm.

   (d) 'I'm afraid there's an awkward gentleman in them, sir'
'Just going to begin'
'Thank you sir'

   (e) There are a number of possible ways of answering this question, though the response should include reference to Mr Winkle falling over, or struggling on the ice.

9. (a) The stranger opened the window when he was alone, and took off his belt, scabbard, his long spurred boots and wig.

   (b) The stranger could see the sea from his window.

   (c) It was the end of the day ('the bugles sounded the last calls of the day').

   (d) There was a box in the saddle bag.

   (e) The stranger was disguised with a wig.

   (f) The stranger had travelled by sea.

   (g) The previous owner of the box had drowned.

   (h) The box had been hidden under the sea.

   (i) The stranger's uncle was the King.

10. (a) There were four squirrels in the nest.

   (b) The mother squirrel first gave a note of warning when Rusty, Hazel and the narrator were sitting in the nest, after she heard footsteps.

   (c) The enemies first attacked after the footsteps stopped just below the squirrels' tree.

   (d) The squirrels stayed in the nest, apart from Hazel who jumped out of the nest only to be caught by her mother and returned to the nest.

   (e) The nest was made of sticks. It was in a pine tree.

   (f) The mother squirrel left the nest because a man appeared below the nest and put his hand out to grab the branch on which the nest was built.

   (g) The squirrels knew that someone was trying to reach them because they heard hob-nailed boots scraping on the tree as they tried to climb up, followed by a man's head appearing below them.

   (h) The enemy was beaten back by mother squirrel biting his finger, making him let go of the branch and fall.

(*i*) In the end the climber managed to catch another branch on his fall so was saved from falling to the ground.

(*j*) The reference to the 'glimpse of red fur' is the first time the reader guesses the story-teller is a squirrel (up to this point it could have been a bird).

11. (*a*) The man telling the story is a steward.

(*b*) The visitor had come from abroad, as he has landed from the sea.

(*c*) John Paul was in an ill humour because the visitor refused to name himself to anyone but the steward, including John Paul.

(*d*) The visitor's behaviour was unusual in that he hid his face, appeared uneasy and refused to disclose his name to anyone but the steward.

(*e*) We know the visitor was not expected because the steward has to ask 'what manner of man' his visitor was and what his name was.

(*f*) (i) 'with no civility of knocking' means John Paul was not polite enough to knock on the door before entering.

(ii) 'sneering at the name of my office' means having a derogatory attitude to the steward because of his more lowly position.

(iii) 'a sore affront' means an insult.

(iv) 'an effusive manner' means in an emotionally forthcoming way.

12. (*a*) The thrush built her nest in a hawthorn bush.

(*b*) The nest was made from moss, wood and clay.

(*c*) By '... and often an intruding guest/ I watched her secret toils from day to day' the poet means that the narrator was often an unwelcome guest to the thrush who would be guarding her eggs closely, but he continued to watch her making the nest and sitting on the eggs until they hatched each day.

(*d*) The line of the poem that best describes the appearance of the thrush's eggs is 'Ink-spotted-over, shells of greeny blue'.

(*e*) The lines from the poem that suggest the eggs hatched and the young birds came out is 'And there I witness, in the sunny hours,/A brood of Nature's minstrels chirp and fly'.

(*f*) 'heath-bells' refers to harebells, which are found on heaths.

'minstrels' means a group of people (or birds in this case!) who sing for a living.

13. (*a*) There are a many ways of answering this question. We'll trust you to mark yourself sensibly! The response should include descriptions of the way the knights were dressed and armed, the fact they were on horseback, a description of audience watching them, the area they were fighting in and the outcome of the fight, including the awarding of the prize to the victorious knight by the 'Queen of Beauty'.

(*b*) Skill in arms was more thought of than learning because men often had to fight for their lands and their lives.

(*c*) The duties of a knight included passing through a course of training in the use of weapons, pledging his loyalty to the king, defending religion, and protecting any lady in danger.

(*d*) Numerous possible answers to this question, e.g.: 'The knights took part in an archery contest.' 'Each knight swore he was loyal to the king.' 'On the knight's shield was a coat-of-arms, by which he could be identified.'

'The fighting arena was enclosed by a fence.'
'The "Queen of Beauty" presided over the sports of the day.'

14. (a) I don't think the sea would ever enter the cave, because when the tide was 'pretty full' the narrator still had to go down the stairs to the water. Also, because the smugglers only move inside the passages in winter because 'a fire could not be seen from the sea there', not because the water submerged the cave.

(b) The smugglers left their caves to light their pipes so the lights could not be seen from the sea.

(c) The writer thinks the smugglers 'could manage very well' in summer because it would still be light anyway so the light of their pipes would not be seen.

(d) (i) 'The tide was pretty full' means that the tide has come in, and is therefore high.

(ii) 'They supped off the remains of the dinner' means the smugglers ate what was left of their evening meal.

(iii) 'Smugglers' means a group of people who illegally imported and exported goods.

15. (a) The men were miners.

(b) They were excited about a pit disaster.

(c) The men were wet and tired.

(d) They had worked over two days and nights.

(e) The men were eager to continue their work.

(f) They were hardly able to walk.

16. (a) It was late afternoon (tea time).

(b) It was winter ('towards the end of the year').

(c) The ducks remind the writer of soldiers drilling because they are marching in line, with their toes out.

(d) The ducks in the yard were making a terrible quacking because the brook had become flooded and muddy due to the unceasing rain, leaving the old white drake stuck.

(e) The meaning of the phrase 'the triangles of their feet' is that ducks' feet are webbed, which makes them look triangular.

(f) Annie guessed that the oldest of the ducks was missing, which would upset the other ducks.

(g) The ducks running in front of them helped the children find out where the cause of the trouble was.

(h) (i) The example the writer gives to show that the drake was a bird of good manners is that he was 'always the last to help himself from the pan of barley-meal'.

   (ii) The example the writer gives to show that the drake was a loving father is that he was 'the first to show fight to a dog or a cock interfering with his family'.

(i) The drake had gone down to the brook because he usually dabbled and searched for tadpoles and caddis-worms there.

(j) The drake was upset because the brook had flooded and he was unaccustomed to such high waters.

(k) The incessant rain had caused the change in the brook.

(l) (i) 'troughs' are the v-shaped containers that animals ate and drank from.

   (ii) 'commotion' means a state of excitement and confusion, often accompanied by lots of noise.

(iii) 'carrying on' refers to excitable behaviour, making noise.

(iv) 'dabble' refers to getting wet by splashing.

17. (*a*) All the animals mentioned in the passage are: squirrel, kitten, monkey, bird, chamois, panther.

   (*b*) The adjectives which describe the squirrel are: beautiful, happy, wonderful, innocent, harmless, playful, grotesque, gentle.

   (*c*) The other being mentioned in the passage are quadrupeds, gnome, fairy, angel, children.

   (*d*) The writer calls it 'the miracle of the forest' because it moves more like a sunbeam than an animal (i.e. because it is so fast and agile).

   (*e*) The writer of the passage is not a good writer. He makes excessive use of adjectives 'so beautiful, so happy, so wonderful . . . Innocent in all his ways, harmless in his food, playful as a kitten' etc., he uses inappropriate similes (e.g. 'grotesque as a gnome'), and inappropriate verbs ('it haunts you, 'looks for you', 'loves you') for a squirrel. General use of florid language ('surpassing the fantastic dexterity of the monkey').

   Other answers acceptable so long as they are appropriate and cite relevant examples.

18. (*a*) victors/winners

   (*b*) illegible

   (*c*) conscientious

   (*d*) silently

   (*e*) innocent

   (*f*) healthy

   (*g*) improving

   (*h*) diminished

(*i*) mischievous

(*j*) library

19. There are numerous possible answers for these, e.g.

Lewis Caroll was an English writer. He wrote the famous *Alice's Adventures in Wonderland* and its sequel *Through the Looking Glass*. As well as being a writer, he was a mathematician, photographer and a clergyman. His real name was Charles Lutwidge Dodgson.

Shylock is a famous Jewish character created by Shakespeare. He appears in the play, *The Merchant of Venice*. Shylock is a moneylender. He demands a 'pound of flesh' from the merchant.

Sherlock Holmes is a fictional character created by Sir Arthur Conan Doyle. Sherlock is a brilliant detective. He has a friend who helps him in his investigations called Dr Watson. Holmes appears in many stories by Conan Doyle, including 'The Adventure of the Speckled Band'.

Scrooge is a character created by Charles Dickens. He appears in the novella *A Christmas Carol*. Scrooge hates Christmas. He is visited by the three spirits of Christmas (past, present and future) who teach him to change his miserly ways.

Peter Pan is the main character in a book of the same name, by J.M. Barrie. Peter Pan is a boy who flies and refuses to grow up. He lives in Neverland with his friends, the Lost Boys. Peter has an enemy called Captain Hook.

'The Song of Hiawatha' is a poem by Henry Longfellow. Hiawatha is a Red Indian [now referred to as Native Americans]. He had a lover called Minnehaha. However Hiawatha becomes Christian and leaves his homeland.

GENERAL INTELLIGENCE/ KNOWLEDGE

1. NEAR – remote
   LIKENESS – difference
   ENLARGE – decrease
   LOOSE – tight
   ARRANGE – disturb
   BEGIN – finish
   AFTER – before
   YOUNG – aged
   LATE – punctual
   FOOT – hand

2. Tom is the best friend

3. (a) 15
   (b) 26
   (c) 23
   (d) 52
   (e) 75
   (f) 21
   (g) 60
   (h) 18

4.

T	C	A
B	H	X
S	E	R

5. (a) The <u>path</u> ran down the <u>boy</u>.
   (b) Jane <u>bird</u> like a <u>flew</u>.
   (c) The <u>swam</u> <u>fish</u> in the sea.

(d) The dog <u>down</u> the cat <u>chased</u> the street.

(e) The <u>writing</u> was <u>teacher</u> on the blackboard.

(f) Jimmie <u>sleeping</u> the <u>stroked</u> cat.

(g) Mother <u>scrub</u> Mary to <u>told</u> the floor.

(h) There were many <u>streets</u> on the <u>people</u>.

(i) Willie had ten or eleven <u>birthday</u> on his <u>letters</u>.

(j) They lay on the <u>birds</u> while the <u>grass</u> flew above them.

(k) The children were <u>long</u> after their <u>hungry</u> walk.

(l) John ran in the <u>cake</u> while James ate <u>race</u> in the refreshment room.

(m) Leaves were <u>trees</u> from the <u>falling</u>.

(n) The child <u>while</u> slept the wind blew.

(o) John wrote his <u>book</u> on his new <u>name</u>.

(p) My cousin is <u>fortnight</u> to stay with me in a <u>coming</u>.

(q) As their mother had a <u>noise</u> they were told not to make a <u>headache</u>.

(r) He <u>read</u> on his glasses and <u>put</u> a book.

(s) John was <u>last</u> of his class <u>top</u> year.

(t) As it was <u>quietly</u> heavily they had to play <u>raining</u> indoors.

(u) The frightened child <u>man</u> away from the angry <u>ran</u>.

(v) The squirrel <u>top</u> up to the <u>climbed</u> of the tree.

(w) Mabel <u>singing</u> round the garden <u>ran</u> at the top of her voice.

(x) <u>Play</u> school the children went to <u>after</u>.

(y) He gets <u>eight</u> when the clock strikes <u>up</u>.

(z) The <u>sock</u> was knitting a <u>mother</u> for her son.

6. (a) herd, shoal, swarm, flock, murder

(b) United States of America, British Broadcasting Corporation, Her/His Majesty's Ship, please turn over, United Nations Organization, Her/His Royal Highness, Member of Parliament

7. Celia Clark
   Sally Smith
   Molly Jones
   Ruth Jones
   Ruth Evans
   Gwen Brown

8. (a) pencil, chalk, <u>ruler</u>, pen.
   (b) velvet, muslin, calico, <u>thread</u>.
   (c) yellow, green, red, <u>colour</u>.
   (d) river, lake, sea, <u>mountain</u>.
   (e) <u>writing</u>, book, story, novel
   (f) milk, <u>drink</u>, water, tea
   (g) book, volume, magazine, <u>print</u>
   (h) carpet, rug, mat, <u>mattress</u>
   (i) skate, <u>stand</u>, slide, slip
   (j) cold, warm, <u>heat</u>, freezing
   (k) policeman, soldier, <u>sailor</u>, airman
   (l) round, <u>shape</u>, square, oblong
   (m) shout, <u>think</u>, speak, whisper
   (n) oak, ash, elm, <u>palm</u>
   (o) sweet, rich, <u>chocolate</u>, sugary
   (p) pen, pencil, <u>paper</u>, crayon
   (q) hammer, <u>plank</u>, chisel, hatchet
   (r) hat, cap, bonnet, <u>scarf</u>

9. Until you are ~~often~~ told to let ~~him~~ go your end of the ~~missing~~ rope, hold it firmly in the left ~~with~~ hand.

10. (*a*) BACK is to FRONT as HEEL is to (SIDE, <u>TOE</u>, PLACE).

(*b*) INK is to PEN as (HAIR, HANDLE, <u>PAINT</u>) is to BRUSH

(*c*) MAN is to CROWD as DROP is to (FALL, FLOCK, <u>WATER</u>).

(*d*) NOTE is to MUSIC as (SENSE, LENGTH, <u>WORD</u>) is to SENTENCE.

(*e*) HOUSE is to MAN as (SHELTER, HOME, <u>HOLE</u>) is to FOX.

11. (*a*) sever; (*b*) duplicate; (*c*) frequently; (*d*) might; (*e*) apparel

12. (*a*) Tom; (*b*) Molly; (*c*) Tom

13. (*a*) iii; (*b*) ii; (*c*) iv

14. (*a*) princess

(*b*) pork

(*c*) cold

(*d*) August

(*e*) trap

(*f*) eight

15. (*a*) banana

(*b*) horse

(*c*) Margaret

(*d*) wardrobe

(*e*) raisins

16. Please note, questions (*a*) and (*d*) were completed for you.

(*b*) 10, 16

    (*c*) 4, 8

    (*e*) 10, 15, 20, 25, 30, 35

    (*f*) 27, 44

    (*g*) 1400, 14,000

17. (*a*) spoon

    (*b*) eye

    (*c*) raspberry

    (*d*) tulip

    (*e*) shears

18. (*a*) happened

    (*b*) sat

    (*c*) discussing

    (*d*) Carter's

    (*e*) when

    (*f*) youngest

    (*g*) dinner

    (*h*) thoroughly

    (*i*) Mr

    (*j*) given

    (*k*) suit

    (*l*) decided

    (*m*) train

    (*n*) son

    (*o*) able

    (*p*) follow

    (*q*) gardener

    (*r*) find

    (*s*) healthy

    (*t*) outdoor

19. (*a*) rustling; (*b*) banging; (*c*) screeching; (*d*) creaking

20. (*a*) Our black cat had a fight with the retriever next door.
    (*b*) The family went to the sea for a swim.
    (*c*) The shepherd stood by the gate and whistled to his dog.
    (*d*) Joan was stung by a bee.
    (*e*) Sailors have to be able to climb.

21. (*a*) somewhat
    (*b*) pigeon
    (*c*) bus
    (*d*) the
    (*e*) rough
    (*f*) book
    (*g*) spade
    (*h*) charm
    (*i*) justice
    (*j*) jug
    (*k*) climbing
    (*l*) blue
    (*m*) sewing

22. (*a*) Susan
    (*b*) 10 marks

23. (*a*) hand
    (*b*) five
    (*c*) toe
    (*d*) short
    (*e*) flock
    (*f*) year

(g) sour
(h) jar
(i) animal
(j) florist

24. (a) pencil, paper
   (b) bracelet, wrist
   (c) elbow, arm
   (d) niece, nephew
   (e) doctor, round
   (f) yellow, lemon
   (g) duke, duchess
   (h) river, stream
   (i) cot, nursery
   (j) musician, concert

25. (a) 64, 128
   (b) 43, 50
   (c) 33, 28
   (d) 23, 30
   (e) 5, 12
   (f) 729, 2187
   (g) 15, 6
   (h) 17, 23

26. (a) barrel, leash, squire, clean, throng
   (b) 26th December

27. (a) 2
   (b) 3
   (c) 4
   (d) 2

    (e) 3

    (f) 3

    (g) 3

    (h) 2

28. (a) 11 ducas

    (b) 7 ducas

    (c) 3 floras

29. (a) Brasted

    (b) Knockholt

    (c) Dunton Green

    (d) Brasted

30. The best answer would be (d).

ACKNOWLEDGEMENTS

The publishers would like to thank Dr Martin Stephen for providing the insightful Foreword, and Colin Rees for supplying the papers from which the questions are taken. Thanks also to Martin Bristow for his ever-excellent design.

Gratitude is also due to the following for supplying the guideline answers to the questions. In alphabetical order:

Silvia Crompton, Anna Marx, and Penny Richardson-White.